The Memoirs of
Helene Kottanner (1439–1440)

Library of Medieval Women   ISSN 1369–9652

Series Editor: Jane Chance

Already published

Christine de Pizan's Letter of Othea to Hector, *Jane Chance*, 1990

The Writings of Margaret of Oingt, Medieval Prioress and Mystic, *Renate Blumenfeld-Kosinski*, 1990

Saint Bride and her Book: Birgitta of Sweden's Revelations, *Julia Bolton Holloway*, 1992

The Memoirs of
Helene Kottanner (1439–1440)

Translated from the German
with Introduction, Interpretative Essay and Notes

Maya Bijvoet Williamson
American University in Cairo

D. S. BREWER

First published 1998
D. S. Brewer, Cambridge

ISBN 0 85991 462 3

D. S. Brewer is an imprint of Boydell & Brewer Ltd
PO Box 9, Woodbridge, Suffolk IP12 3DF, UK
and of Boydell & Brewer Inc.
PO Box 41026, Rochester, NY 14604–4126, USA

A catalogue record for this book is available
from the British Library

Library of Congress Cataloging-in-Publication Data
Williamson, Maya Bijvoet.
    [Denkwürdigkeiten der Helene Kottannerin (1439–1440). English]
    The memoirs of Helene Kottanner (1439–1440) : translated from the
German with introduction, interpretative essay and notes / Maya
Bijvoet Williamson.
        p.   cm. – (Library of medieval women)
    Includes bibliographical references and index.
    ISBN 0–85991–462–3 (alk. paper)
    1. Albert II, Holy Roman Emperor, 1397–1439. 2. László V, King of
Hungary and Bohemia, 1440–1457. 3. Women – Hungary – History – Middle
Ages, 500–1500. 4. Holy Crown of Hungary. 5. Kottannerin, Helene.
I. Kottannerin, Helene. II. Title. III. Series.
DD172.K6713W55 1998
943.9'03'092 – dc21
[B]   97–37483

This publication is printed on acid-free paper

Printed in Great Britain by
Athenæum Press Ltd, Gateshead, Tyne & Wear

Contents

For Herb, David and Sarah

Preface

On the night of 20 February 1440, an Austrian woman in the service of Queen Elizabeth of Hungary named Helene, or Elena, Kottanner (sometimes spelled Quottanner) and an unnamed Hungarian collaborator broke into a closely guarded vault at the royal stronghold of Plintenburg and secretly removed from its heavily sealed casing the Holy Crown of Saint Stephen.[1] The next day, they smuggled the crown out of the castle hidden in a pillow and on a sled rushed their precious booty to the queen, who within an hour of the crown's arrival at her castle of Komorn, some sixty-five kilometers to the west, bore a son, Ladislaus Posthumous.[2] Three months later, the little baby boy was crowned King of Hungary in the coronation city Stuhlweissenburg.[3]

These events, their historical context, and immediate political consequences are related with remarkable vividness and poignancy in a small manuscript preserved in the Austrian National Library in Vienna. Known as *Die Denkwurdigkeiten der Helene Kottannerin* (*The Memoirs of Helene Kottanner*), it contains the eye-witness account of Queen Elizabeth's adventurous servant and may be considered the oldest memoir written by a woman in the German language. It is also one of the oldest known pieces of historical prose authored by a woman.

With a clear sense of the importance of fact and detail, a solid understanding of late-medieval Hungarian laws and political traditions, knowledge of human nature, and insight into the principles of narrative development, characterization, and audience manipulation, Helene Kottanner paints an absorbing picture of the period as she tells of individual destinies caught in the movement of history. In the process, she

---

1 Elizabeth (1409–1442), the daughter of Sigmund of Luxembourg. She married Albert V, Duke of Austria, a Habsburg, in 1422 and became Queen of Hungary in 1438. Plintenburg is the German name for the Hungarian fortress Visegrad, forty-two kilometers north of Pest on the Danube. Stephen I (997–1038) was crowned with a crown sent by Pope Sylvester II. His title "Apostolic King" was used by all subsequent Hungarian kings. He suppressed paganism, encouraged trade and became patron saint of Hungary, canonized in 1078. Whether or not the Holy Crown is the same crown that was sent to St. Stephen by Pope Sylvester is a matter of debate. See introduction, 18.

2 Komorn: Hungarian Komárom. Ladislaus Posthumous was born on 21 February 1440, son of Elizabeth and her husband Albert, who had died on 27 October 1439.

3 Hungarian Székesfehérvár, south of Budapest, where traditionally all Hungarian kings were crowned.

provides a rare, personal record of the predicaments of two women, the queen and herself, in the face of political pressures, treason, and threats to their life. While "seeking the woman in late-medieval and Renaissance writings," to borrow the title of a recent collection of feminist scholarship, is difficult because of the masculinist perspective in most texts dating from that period, the paucity of female authored texts, and the questionable referentiality of all literary texts, Helene Kottanner's eyewitness account has a factuality and "reality value" rarely found in medieval historiographical writing.[4] It is an ego-document which, although not devoid of distortions, fictionalizing, or ideological coloring, nevertheless confronts the reader in a strikingly direct manner with certain significant moments in the life of two late-medieval women, one a widowed queen, the other a married "servant," both mothers, who are shown to wield power and influence, balance personal and professional considerations, and outwit the men who oppose the queen. The theater of action is Hungary, a part of Europe much neglected by Western scholars, including scholars studying women in the Middle Ages and the Renaissance.[5]

The manuscript, Codex 2920 in the Viennese National Library, consists of sixteen heavily damaged leaves written on both sides. The first two pages are very difficult to read, and on the last page the narrative abruptly breaks off in the middle of a sentence. Whether the present manuscript is the original or a copy has not been sufficiently established.[6] Nor do we know whether the narrator ever completed her story, or how much more of the political events involving Queen Elizabeth and her son she might have covered. Since the initials of Helene Kottanner's name are in most instances written in by a second hand, some commentators have questioned Kottanner's authorship.[7] Others surmise that the author left out her name for reasons of safety. However, this is inconsistent with other information provided in the text; the name of Kottanner's husband, for example, is mentioned (p. 49). Some consider that a middle-class

4   Sheila Fisher and Janet E. Halley, eds., *Seeking the Woman in Late Medieval and Renaissance Writings: Essays in Feminist Contextual Criticism* (Knoxville: Univ. of Tennessee Press, 1989), 1–17.
5   Eastern Europe, like Iberia and Scandinavia, has not received much attention from Western feminist historians studying women in the Middle Ages and Renaissance. See introduction by Susan Mosher Stuart to *Women in Medieval History and Historiography*, ed. Susan Mosher Stuart (Philadelphia: Univ. of Pennsylvania Press, 1987), xv.
6   Karl, Mollay, ed., *Die Denkwürdigkeiten der Helene Kottannerin 1439–1440* (Vienna: Österreichischer Bundesverlag, 1971), 72.
7   Mollay, 72–73.

woman like Helene Kottanner probably did not know how to write and therefore must have dictated her recollections to "a scholarly feather."[8]

Although Helene Kottanner's contemporaries were aware that the Holy Crown had been stolen from the Plintenburg stronghold, the actual circumstances of the abduction remained unknown, even to the queen, until Helene Kottanner revealed them in her *Memoirs*. The history of the manuscript, however, is completely shrouded in darkness until 1834, when an Hungarian historian, Johann Czéch, reported about it to the Hungarian Academy of Sciences.[9] The first published edition of the text dates from 1846.[10] Historians then began to compare Kottanner's account with other sources documenting this period of Hungarian history and were able to identify the author. Parts of the text were included in Gustav Freytag's highly popular *Bilder aus der deutschen Vergangenheit* (*Images from the German Past*) of 1866, which made the story accessible to a much wider readership.[11] Yet Helene Kottanner's narrative has remained virtually unknown.[12] I know of only one, unpublished, rendition of the text into modern German and am not aware of any translations into other languages, not even into Hungarian.[13]

The present English translation is based on an excellent, extensively documented and conscientiously edited transcription of the manuscript, first published in 1965, by the Hungarian historian Karl Mollay.[14] Mollay discusses at length Kottanner's motivation for writing, or dictating, the story, and the rationale of the empty spaces where the author's name was partially or fully written in by another hand. He also stresses the importance of the document for Hungarian legal history and points out the one serious inaccuracy in the text, namely when Kottanner insists that not only the Holy Crown but also the coronation insignia – the apple or orb, the scepter, and the legate staff – were carried around in the coronation

---

8   Mollay, 92. Herbert Zeman postulates an arrangeur, who rewrote and considerably modified the account dictated by the simple burgher woman but preserved her expressive language in many descriptive passages. "Österreichische Literatur: Zwei Studien," *Jahrbuch der Grillparzer-Gesellschaft*, 3:8 (1970): 17–18.

9   Mollay, 69.

10   *Aus den Denkwürdigkeiten der Helene Kottannerin*, ed. Engelmann (Leipzig: 1846).

11   Mollay, 71 n. 10.

12   There is one historical novel for children, Maria Kilényi's *Könnyek és Korona* (*Tears and Crown*), published in Budapest in 1947, which is based on Kottanner's *Memoirs*, and a small segment of the *Memoirs* appears in Heimito von Doderer's novel *Die Dämonen* (1956). Outside Hungary and Austria, however, Kottanner's text seems to be virtually unknown.

13   By the Austrian novelist Heimito von Doderer.

14   *Die Denkwürdigkeiten der Helene Kottannerin (1439–1440)*, ed. Karl Mollay, first published in *Jahrbuch Arrabona*, 7 (Györ: 1965): 237–296. I used the 1971 edition published by the Österreichischer Bundesverlag, in Wiener Neudrücke, Band 2.

procession, although these had in fact stayed in the treasure vault of the Plintenburg fortress.[15]

As a historian, Mollay naturally focuses primarily on the text's historical aspects, its factual accuracy, and the geographical, political, sociological, anthropological and medical information Kottanner provides. However, there remain a number of neglected areas: on the one hand, the text's literary aspects, particularly its genre and the narrative techniques employed, and on the other hand, the question of the text's female authorship: "That it is a woman who acts and reports here, and the way she acts and reports, constitutes the special attraction of this text," observes one of Mollay's reviewers, and I concur.[16] In fact, I would argue that from a historical as well as literary perspective the female authorship of the *Memoirs* is of primary significance.

In the translation, I have attempted to remain faithful to the atmosphere and rhythm of the original in early new high German, preserving the verbal and phrasal repetitions characteristic both of Helene Kottanner's text and of medieval prose in general. I have also preserved her largely paratactic sentence structure so reminiscent of oral narration and adjusted the punctuation only for the sake of clarity. The division into paragraphs is mine entirely; in the original, there are no titles, chapter headings or subdivisions of any kind. Moreover, following Karl Mollay's practice in the transcription, I have indicated in brackets the exact dates of the events as they have been verified by modern historians.

Probably because Helene Kottanner could understand, but did not speak, let alone read or write, Hungarian, Hungarian place and family names in the manuscript are spelled phonetically, as they may have sounded to a German speaker at the time. To facilitate matters for the English reader, I have used as much as possible modern English equivalents – for first names for example – or else the modern German or Hungarian forms. Wherever Kottanner used the German version of Hungarian place names, I have done so too, while providing the Hungarian name in a note. That there existed German names for most of the Hungarian towns and villages mentioned by Helene Kottanner should not surprise us, for in Buda and elsewhere there were sizable German populations at this time.

Perhaps on account of the heavy damage marring the first two pages of the manuscript and hence the editor's difficulty in reconstructing them, the beginning of the text contains a few rough spots that make for

---

[15] See the essay following the translation, 55–56.
[16] Ingo Reiffenstein's review of Mollay's edition in *Sprachkunst* 4 (1973) 1–2: 164. My translation.

awkward reading. Yet the story quickly gains coherence and momentum, almost as if the narrator's resolve or self-confidence increased as the story took shape. The rambling formlessness of the concluding sentences, by contrast, may signal Kottanner's discomfiture at the unraveling of her queen's fortune or, perhaps more likely, alarm or pressure to complete the story and quickly include what information she still wanted to convey. In keeping with medieval prose in general, there is a certain amount of repetitiveness, a certain monotony, but there are also interesting vignettes portraying aspects of life at court and on the road, moving family scenes, the hardships which arduous journeys and lengthy rituals impose on the infant king, and the lively character sketches of the two women, particularly of Helene Kottanner herself who, in spite of protestations to the contrary, clearly is the heroine of the story. Hence these *Memoirs* constitute both a delightful and moving ancestor of the historical novel and a document of prime value for women's history.

Parts of the translation and sections of my text appeared in slightly different form in *Women of the Renaissance and Reformation*, edited by Katharina M. Wilson (Athens: University of Georgia Press, 1987), and are reprinted by permission. I am grateful to the Dean of the College of Liberal Arts and Sciences of the University of Colorado at Colorado Springs for a research grant allowing me to devote part of the summer of 1986 to the translation.

Introduction

Biographical Information

Though researchers have been able to identify and locate the historical Helene Kottanner, they have been able to do little more than that. In fact, all we know is that Helene Kottanner was probably born in the year 1400 in the Austrian town of Ödenburg.[1] Her father, Peter Wolfram, belonged to the lower nobility and was an official in the service of West Hungarian lords. She married the Hungarian patrician Peter Szekeles, a prominent citizen and later, for at least thirteen years, mayor of Ödenburg. About a year after his death in 1431, she married Johann Kottanner, chamberlain of the provost of the Viennese cathedral, her junior by some years.[2] The couple had several children, one of whom, Katharina, is mentioned in the *Memoirs* (p. 51).

When and exactly in what capacity Helene Kottanner came to be employed by Queen Elizabeth we do not know, but there is evidence that she was at Albert's court in Vienna in 1436.[3] Since the little Elizabeth was born in that year, Helene Kottanner may well have been hired specifically to take care of the newborn; according to the *Memoirs* it was Helene Kottanner who "raised" the little princess (p. 51). Commentators variously refer to Helene Kottanner as "wet-nurse," "nurse," "chambermaid," or "governess."[4] But Kottanner makes it clear that she was all that and much more, not of noble birth like the queen's ladies-in-waiting – several of whom she identifies by name – but much closer to the queen and actually much more influential than these noble women.

Helene Kottanner has been discussed as a very early and modest predecessor of the pompous and frivolous chambermaids who later became famous for their literary confessions: women like Madame de Motteville, Madame de Hausset, Madame de Pompadour, and Mademoiselle d'Avrillon, chambermaid of Napoleon's wife, Joséphine de Bauhar-

---

1   Historians first thought that Helene Kottanner was originally from Siebenburg in Saxonia. The question is elucidated in Mollay, 76–77.
2   Cf. Mollay, 77–78.
3   Cf. Mollay, 78.
4   See, for example, Erik Fugedi, *Kings, Bishops, Nobles and Burghers in Medieval Hungary*, ed. J. M. Bak (London: Variorum, 1986) 1: 159; 175; 179.

nais.[5] More importantly, however, she is an early representative of a particular group of women employed at the European courts, women of humble or patrician origin, whose position at such courts gave them privileges but also responsibilities unknown to other women of their class. Although much research has been done lately on the professional activities of women in the past, the kind of work performed by women like Kottanner has not received much attention, either because, as I will discuss in some detail later, courts and elites have been unpopular topics lately, or, and this is perhaps more likely, because as opposed to the male professions, the activities of women, at the courts as elsewhere, were multifarious and therefore elude easy definition.[6] Hence perhaps our difficulty in finding an adequate professional label for Helene Kottanner who, though she came from a relatively simple social background, occupied an important post at the court of King Albert of Hungary. She was not only in charge of the queen's wardrobe and the material well-being of the ladies-in-waiting, she was also entrusted with the education of the king's children, gave council and was listened to, had a considerable impact on Queen Elizabeth's decisions, and was sent on a highly danger-ous secret mission. In other words, the woman who portrays herself in these pages had a wide range of tasks and responsibilities.

Since, in the Middle Ages, as later on, to be a woman meant first and foremost to be a wife and mother, and since virtually all early, and much later, writing by women manifests a conflict or unresolvable division between the author's sense of responsibility to her family, on the one hand, and her own personal or professional occupations, on the other, it is surprising that the female narrator of these late medieval *Memoirs* should focus exclusively on her professional duties, saying little or nothing about her children or her husband, Johann Kottanner, although he too was employed at Albert's court.[7] They had both followed the king from

5   Alice Wengraf, "Aus den Denkwürdigkeiten der Helene Kottanner," *Ungarische Rund-schau* 3:8 (1970): 438–441.

6   For recent research on the professional lives of women in the Middle Ages and the Renaissance, see for example: Judith M. Bennett et al., eds., *Sisters and Workers in the Middle Ages* (Chicago: Univ. of Chicago Press, 1989); Judith M. Bennett, "History that Stands Still: Women's Work in the European Past," *Feminist Studies* 14, no. 2 (Summer 1988): 269–283; Barbara A. Hanawalt, *Women and Work in Preindustrial Europe* (Bloom-ington: Indiana Univ. Press, 1986); David Herlihy, *Opera Muliebra: Women and Work in Medieval Europe* (Philadelphia: Temple Univ. Press, 1990); Martha C. Howell, *Women, Production and Patriarchy in Late Medieval Cities* (Chicago: Univ. of Chicago Press, 1986); Merry E. Wiesner, *Working Women in Renaissance Germany* (New Brunswick: Rutgers Univ. Press, 1986); Erika Uitz, *Women in the Medieval Towns* (London: Barrie and Jenkins).

7   Basically, medieval women had only two options: to be married carnally, to a husband, or spiritually, to God. Cf. Ross S. Kraemer, "The Conversion of Women to Ascetic Forms of Christianity," in *Sisters and Workers in the Middle Ages*, 198–207. About this conflict in

Vienna to Hungary in April 1439. To judge by Helene Kottanner's independent manner, it seems unlikely that she needed, or indeed would have bothered to try to obtain, her husband's approval to go on the dangerous mission, even if the extreme secrecy of the plan had not made it inadvisable for her to tell him about it. But she probably had his support.

According to a charter of March 1452, János Hunyadi, Governor of Hungary, granted the Kottanners the royal property Kisfalud near Pressburg as reward for their services to the infant king, who reigned as Ladislaus V from 1452 until his untimely death in 1457.[8] However, the couple were apparently unable to take full possession of their property until 1466 or even 1470.[9] Helene Kottanner's *Memoirs* chronicle the precise nature and significance of the couple's services.

Historical Background

Queen Elizabeth's husband, Albert II, the first Habsburg on the Hungarian throne, died on 27 October 1439, six months after moving his court to Hungary. After his death, as Helene Kottanner tells the story, Hungary's leading nobles desired a king who could ward off invasions threatened by the Turks. They urged Albert's widow, thirty-one years of age and five months pregnant, to marry Wladislaus III, King of Poland, who was then sixteen.[10] But Elizabeth, who was strong-willed and ambitious and had been raised for the throne by her father, Sigmund of Luxembourg, had no desire to yield or share power.[11] Since Albert had no male heir at the time of his death, Elizabeth's hope was focused on her unborn child. Her physicians had predicted that it would be a boy. However, since she could not openly oppose the wishes of the Hungarian magnates whose support she needed, she nominally agreed to marry "the Pole," as Helene Kottanner almost always calls him, while secretly plotting to get in her possession the Holy Crown, which Albert, along with the queen's crown and all the royal insignia, had brought to the Plintenburg stronghold in the beginning of July 1439.

The sudden death of the Bishop of Gran, keeper of the crowns, had necessitated their removal to a safe place, and Helene Kottanner, with the little princess on her arm, had stood by and looked on as the crowns and

---

female writing, see Domna Stanton's introductory chapter in *The Female Autograph*, ed. Domna C. Stanton (Chicago: Univ. of Chicago Press, 1987), 13.

8 Cf. Mollay, 71. Pressburg is Bratislava. Ladislaus Posthumous, only 17 when he died on 23 November 1457, may have been poisoned.

9 Cf. Mollay, 72.

10 I.e. Wladislaus Jagiellonczyk, born 1424, not a relative.

11 Sigmund of Luxembourg, who died in 1437, was King of Hungary and German Emperor. As his only child and natural heir to the throne, Elizabeth steered her own course and displayed considerable political ambition even during Albert's lifetime.

insignia, in the presence of Albert, Elizabeth, and major nobles of the country, were placed in the vault and entrusted to the care of the new crown keeper, Count George of Saint George and Posing.[12]

Albert had been designated by his father-in-law Sigmund to succeed him in Hungary and Bohemia, and the Hungarian lords had duly elected him while stipulating that he should defend the country with all his forces and not accept the imperial crown. He had been a conscientious and able leader and had organized the army to campaign against the Turks.[13] His death, of dysentery, after less than two years on the throne, caused a dynastic crisis.

Yet his funeral, in Stuhlweissenburg, is not mentioned in Kottanner's *Memoirs*. Interested only in the queen and her efforts to hold on to power, Kottanner briefly describes the circumstances surrounding Albert's death and then concentrates on the Holy Crown and on her own role as a devoted servant and accomplice of her mistress.

Early in November 1439 she was again an eyewitness when the queen, alarmed by rumors that Albert shortly before his death had taken advantage of one of her numerous absences to recover the crown and hide it elsewhere, personally ascertained the falseness of these allegations and, reluctant to let the treasure out of her sight, moved the crowns into her own bedchamber. That night, a fire broke out in the room which almost destroyed the crowns. The following day, the crowns were returned to the vault and the doors and locks covered with multiple seals. Elizabeth then appointed her cousin Ladislaus Garai keeper of the crowns and commander of Plintenburg.[14] Then the court traveled to Komorn, and after secret deliberations with her most loyal advisors Elizabeth ordered Helene Kottanner to journey back to the Plintenburg stronghold and abduct the Holy Crown. Kottanner shows that she did this with courage and intelligence although, as her fearful thoughts and fervid prayers during the night of the theft suggest, perhaps not entirely without a guilty conscience.

Why Queen Elizabeth selected Helene Kottanner to execute her dangerous plan is not difficult to understand. Kottanner is depicted as bright, trustworthy, and endowed with a good measure of common sense. A mother herself and older than Elizabeth, she felt protective and maternal

12 Gran: H. Esztergóm. Archbishop George Pelóczi had crowned Albert on 1 January 1438 and thereafter kept the Holy Crown as well as the queen's crown and the royal insignia in his castle at Gran. As soon as Albert heard of the bishop's death, he went to Gran to take possession of the treasure.

13 C. A. Macartney, *Hungary* (Edinburgh: Univ. of Edinburgh Press, 1953), 51.

14 His mother and Queen Elizabeth's mother, Barbara, were sisters, both daughters of Count Hermann Cillei.

toward the young widow. As a personal assistant to the queen, she was frequently sent on errands, so that her sudden arrival at the Plintenburg castle, under the pretext of fetching the ladies-in-waiting who had stayed behind, raised no suspicion. Moreover, she was also intimately familiar with the interior of the Plintenburg castle and had seen with her own eyes where and how the crown was kept.

With the Holy Crown safely in her possession, Elizabeth, to secure the legitimate rights of her son, wanted Ladislaus crowned at the earliest opportunity.[15] The royal household celebrated the boy's birth with bonfires and a ride in lighted boats on the Danube, and the next day, on 22 February 1440, Ladislaus Posthumous was baptized in the chapel of the castle at Komorn. The Polish faction, however, remained firm in its wish to see Wladislaus III (called Ulaszlo by the Hungarians) king of Hungary and insisted again that Elizabeth remarry as soon as possible.[16] Lords and prelates flocked to Komorn to pay their respects to the queen and her young son, but many, says Kottanner, were insincere and in reality unwilling to acknowledge the child's claims to the throne. Elizabeth was well aware of this. Together with her confidante, she watched from the walls of the castle as on her command the leaders of the opposition were surprised and arrested in a hamlet across the river where they had gathered for secret *pourparlers*. Then hasty preparations were made for the child's coronation, and behind the locked doors of the chapel Helene Kottanner quickly sewed the future king's minute ceremonial dress. On 12 May, Elizabeth and a large train of state and church dignitaries summoned for the occasion set out for Stuhlweissenburg, where they arrived two days later. On 15 May, the day of Pentecost, the twelve-week-old child was confirmed, knighted, and anointed king.

In the last part of the story, broadening the political perspective, Helene Kottanner expands on the opposition and hatred between the queen's German-Bohemian associates and the Hungarian magnates who supported the Polish king. She describes the Hungarian people's fear of Elizabeth's soldiers, peasants fleeing their villages as the queen's retinue approaches, conflict and strife between her Hungarian and German soldiers, and citizens refusing the royal family entrance into their town. Receiving word of conspiracies aiming to end the life of her son, the queen decides to move her family from Stuhlweissenburg to Raab.[17] There it is

---

[15] As Helene Kottanner explains, Hungarian tradition dictated that coronations be held on major holidays. Elizabeth chose the earliest possible date, 15 May, Pentecost.

[16] If Wladislaus married Elizabeth, dynastic continuity was assured as well. Cf. János M. Bak, *Königtum und Stände in Ungarn im 14.–16. Jahrhundert* (Wiesbaden: Franz Steiner Verlag, 1973), 41.

[17] Raab: H. Gyor.

thought wiser to separate the royal family and to send the little king to
Ödenburg under the military protection of Ulrich of Eitzing. While
Johann Kottanner is assigned to the retinue of the little princess, his wife
is given a more important assignment, namely to accompany the little
king and take care of him. She does this, albeit reluctantly, she says,
leaving her own children in the care of her husband.

Upon their arrival in Ödenburg, Ladislaus' attendants learn that the
Polish king has captured Elizabeth's most loyal supporter, Count Ulrich
Cillei, as well as her cousin, Ladislaus Garai, and the Bishop of Gran.
With their help Wladislaus hopes to effect his own crowning as King of
Hungary, for since no one except Kottanner and her anonymous helper
knows exactly what happened, these men suspect that Elizabeth may have
cheated and that the Holy Crown has remained in the treasure vault,
because all the locks and seals on the door are still intact. Here the
narrative stops abruptly.

We have to turn to other sources to learn that the Polish Wladislaus
was crowned two months later, on 17 July 1440, having declared the little
boy's coronation null and void.[18] Since Queen Elizabeth had taken the
Holy Crown with her to Vienna and there pawned it to Frederick III, it
was not available for Wladislaus' coronation. Instead, his supporters used
a new crown fashioned especially for the occasion in addition to the
Hungarian regalia which had remained in the treasure vault of the Plintenburg.

Historiographical and Literary Context

Helene Kottanner probably did not voluntarily interrupt her story in the
middle of a sentence, but whether she discontinued the narrative for
political or other reasons, we do not know. Mollay and other commentators agree that the manuscript probably dates from sometime between the
death of Queen Elizabeth, on 19 December 1442, and the death of
Ladislaus Posthumous, on 23 November 1457. Mollay feels that it was
most likely written around 1450, shortly before Hunyadi officially
granted the Kottanners the property near Pressburg.[19] On paleographical
and linguistic grounds, the manuscript can certainly date from that time.

As I indicated earlier, much conjecture revolves around the rationale
for the spaces left blank throughout the manuscript for the narrator's
name. Five times her first initial is written in by a first hand. Three times

---

18 János Bak, "The Late Medieval Period," in *A History of Hungary*, eds. Peter Sugar et al.
(Bloomington: Indiana Univ. Press, 1990), 63.
19 Cf. Mollay, 72; 91–92.

both initials appear in the same hand, while in five other places her whole name is written in by a second hand. The names of her Hungarian collaborator and his servant have been left out. There are many spelling mistakes, words missing, unnecessary repetitions, and corrections by a second hand, which have led some critics to believe that what we have here is a copy rather than the original.[20] The writing is regular and practiced. Whether it is from the hand of Helene Kottanner herself or of a professional scribe cannot be verified.

Since female literacy was very low in the Middle Ages, it was not uncommon for a woman to resort to a scribe if she wanted to commit something to paper. Even the most prolific of medieval women writers, the mystics, frequently relied on the pen of others to relate their religious experiences and visions. (Incidentally, male literacy being low as well, it was not uncommon for men to rely on scribes either.) But the inability to write or even read was not necessarily an impediment to serious authorship. Margery Kempe, a contemporary of Helene Kottanner's and author of the oldest female autobiography in English, *The Booke of Margery Kempe* (1436–1438), was illiterate and therefore had to dictate her story to others. She nevertheless took her role as a writer very seriously and kept re-working her texts incessantly.[21]

Kottanner's account has all the features of an oral narration and may well have been dictated. This impression is reinforced by injunctions in the text such as: "But hear now," or "Listen now." On the other hand, the use of such injunctions is also a standard technique in contemporary chronicles, for example in Jakob Unrest's slightly later *Austrian Chronicle*, which may indicate that Helene Kottanner was familiar with such writing.[22]

Her story, however, has an unmistakable feminine focus, bespeaking the observing eye and sensibility of a woman. This suggests that if Kottanner dictated her story, whoever took it down for her must have recorded the spoken word with fidelity. As opposed to her contemporary Ulrich von Lapitz, for example, whose autobiography stresses activities and ambitions of concern to men – tournaments, campaigns, hunting – Helene Kottanner shows compassion for pillaged peasants, understands the common people's fear of Elizabeth's approaching army, and limits her

---

[20] Cf. Mollay, 91–92.
[21] See Mary G. Mason's discussion of Margery Kempe in "The Other Voice: Autobiographies of Women Writers," in *Autobiography: Essays Theoretical and Critical*, ed. James Olney (Princeton: Princeton Univ. Press, 1980), 209–210.
[22] About Unrest, see 9; 12–13.

observations mostly, though not exclusively, to her own domain, the women's quarters.[23]

From an historiographical point of view, her eyewitness report is a valuable, highly accurate source of information on this episode in Hungarian history. It is much more precise and truthful than other contemporary texts dealing with this period, such as János Thuróczy's *Hungarian Chronicle*.[24] Moreover, Kottanner provides interesting details on the inner arrangement of the Visegrad stronghold, sheds new light on contemporary medical practice and theory, explains legal and cultural traditions, describes how the royal family traveled and lived – their vestments, ornaments, utensils, rituals and ceremonies – and imparts a sense of the tremendous importance of royal crowns and insignia in this society steeped in feudalism yet challenging the right of hereditary kingship.

In comparison with other historiographical writings produced at the time, in Latin as well as in German, Kottanner's vocabulary is rich, her language vivid and varied, her spelling exceptionally uniform. As a literary text, her work has been judged superior to the writings of the humanists Aeneas Sylvius Piccolomini (1405–1461) and Johann Dlugosz (1415–1480) and much more expressive and lively than the comparable *Leben Konig Sigmunds* (*Life of King Sigmund*) by the merchant Eberhard Windecke.[25] But in order to fully appreciate Kottanner's *Memoirs* as history and qua text we must place the text in its proper historiographical and literary context.

Few women wrote in the Middle Ages and of those who did very few wrote secular prose. Instead, religion being the only other proper field of activity for women besides marriage and maternity, women mostly concentrated on religious writing. There is a considerable body of religious texts by female mystics, and nuns occasionally wrote down the legend of a venerated saint, the life of a beloved mother superior, or small-scale histories of their own order, as for example Hroswith's history of her abbey at Gandersheim, written before 968, or *The Life of St. Adelaide* by the nun Bertha, written in the first half of the eleventh century.[26] This trend prevailed throughout Europe until well into the sixteenth century, with Santa Theresa in Spain and in Hungary the Dominican nun Lea

23 Kottanner's characteristically feminine focus is discussed in greater detail by Alice Wengraf, 441.
24 See my discussion, 9–12.
25 Wengraf, 438; Mollay, 83.
26 On women as writers of history, see the chapter by Natalie Zemon Davis in *Beyond Their Sex: Learned Women of the European Past*, ed. Patricia H. Labalme (New York, 1980), 160–161.

Raskai, author of a vita of St. Margaret.[27] While the development of the middle class, and of the towns and cities, in Europe increased travel to other parts of the world, and while the crusades, in particular, gave rise to numerous other prose writings, in Latin as well as increasingly also in the vernacular – from town chronicles and national histories to diaries, notebooks, memoirs and travelogues – women had no part in this production. Hence, Margery Kempe's autobiography of 1436 is an anomaly. So are the *Alexiad* of the eleventh-century Byzantine princess Anna Comnena and the works of Christine de Pisan, who produced a body of texts astonishing in size and range, including romances, literary criticism, philosophy, and a *Life of King Charles V* of France.

Speculating about the difficulties facing a would-be female historian in the past, Natalie Zemon Davis postulated as primary requirements that the prospective female historian, like her male counterpart, should have access to archives and materials and be able to familiarize herself with the accepted modes of historical discourse and the rules for ordering and recording historical data; she should have a sense of connection with the areas of public life considered suitable for treatment in writing, and be able to count on an audience which would take her seriously.[28] For the vast majority of medieval women, confined to the domestic sphere or to the convent, this was impossible. Only rarely did an occasional noblewoman, such as the princess Anna Comnena, or women who witnessed, or were involved in, public life at major courts, such as Christine de Pisan and also Helene Kottanner, venture to record their experiences in writing. Like Anna Comnena, Helene Kottanner needed no access to records or documents, for she herself played a pivotal part in the historical process and saw with her own eyes most of what she describes. She very likely was familiar with the modes of contemporary history writing, was herself involved, be it indirectly, in several areas of public life, and meant to be taken seriously by her readers, although her intentions probably were not primarily historiographical. As I will discuss in greater detail later, unusual public and private circumstances prompted Kottanner's unique venture into secular historical prose.

That she had some familiarity with the prevailing forms of contemporary historical writing is suggested by similarities, in organization, structure, style, language and vocabulary, between her text and that of well-known chronicles of the period, such as the Hungarian and Austrian chronicles of Jakob Unrest, written in German, and János Thuróczy's

---

27 See the chapter on Lea Raskái in *Women Writers of the Renaissance and Reformation*, ed. K. M. Wilson (Athens: Univ. of Georgia Press, 1987), 435–446.
28 Natalie Zemon Davis, "Gender and Genre: Women as Historical Writers, 1400–1820," in *Beyond Their Sex*, 154–156.

Latin *Chronicle of the Hungarians*. These histories are somewhat posterior to the *Memoirs*, but they rely on much older sources which were in
circulation in Kottanner's day. Because they include the historical events
treated in the *Memoirs*, it may be useful to refer to them.

Thuróczy's *History of the Hungarian People up to the Rule of King
Matthias*, printed in 1488, was intended to fill the need for a written
account of the events of the last hundred years or so which had been
preserved only in chancellory documents and the memories of contemporaries. After John Küküllei's *Gesta* of the reign of King Louis the Great
(1342–1382), no one had provided a systematic written account of the
main events of the century that followed. Although there apparently was
much interest in these events – and history writing was in fact the only
secular genre that received attention in Hungary from the eleventh century
on – this historical interest seems to have expressed itself at this time only
in conversation and oral narration. The *Buda Chronicle*, the first-known
printed work in Hungarian, published in 1473, contains material from the
old chronicles up to 1382 but virtually nothing from the ensuing century.[29]

This may well be due, at least in part, to the fact that literacy spread
very late in Hungary, so that even in Thuróczy's day, in the closing
decades of the fifteenth century, the vast majority of the Hungarian
nobility were unable to sign their own name. Oral testimony carried the
weight of truth, and eyewitness reports and personal recollections were
used as a reliable basis for judicial decisions.[30]

Hence, before the Renaissance flowering of the court of King Matthias
Corvinus (1458–1490) attracted foreign scholars and poets to Hungary,
the country had no literate culture to speak of. Literacy, for the most part,
meant competence in Latin, which was the language of administration,
used for royal charters and other notarial and administrative documents.
The clerks and administrators of the chancelleries and courts of justice
usually came from families of the lower nobility who had the means to
educate their sons but were unable to offer them property or other
professional prospects.

Thuróczy belonged to this class. Born around 1435, he worked as a
clerk and later judge all his life, mostly in Buda. Encouraged by his
superiors at the Court of Royal Appeals there, he began writing his
chronicle around 1480, a task no doubt facilitated by his access to charters
and other documents of historical significance.

His *History* consists of four parts covering different periods and, with

---

29 See Pál Engel, foreword to János Thuróczy's *Chronicle of the Hungarians*, trans. Frank
Mantello (Bloomington: Indiana Univ. Press, 1991), 6–7; 12.

30 See Erik Fügedi, " 'Verba volant . . .': Oral Culture and Literacy among the Medieval
Hungarian Nobility," in *Kings, Bishops, Nobles*, 6: 1–25.

the exception of the third part, relies heavily on older chronicles. Part 4 consists of the *Gesta* of John Küküllei which Thuróczy adopted in their entirety. In Part 3, however, he recounts the events of his own lifetime on the basis of personal recollections, information provided by contemporaries, and a number of royal charters. Since in Hungary, unlike anywhere else in Europe, these charters contained long narrative parts, they could almost serve as chronicles.[31] Book 3 is the part that concerns us here. It starts in 1387 and goes up to the time of writing.

In the Preface Thuróczy states as his purpose: "to ensure that events which someone's pen has not written down may not disappear from the records of mankind."[32] Then, in the fashion typical of ancient as well as medieval writers, he employs a humility topos, stressing his own modest qualifications as a writer and the mediocrity of his Latin. The ensuing narrative is ordered chronologically, recording the deeds of the great personalities of the period, which ordering is underpinned, in equally characteristic fashion, by reference to all the holidays and feasts in the Church calendar, the natural dating system for medieval people.

But it becomes clear very soon that Thuróczy is not merely a "recorder" of the deeds of men but writes under the influence of strong political views. For example, he takes side with the Polish faction and the Hunyadian dynasty, the enemies of Queen Elizabeth, and is highly critical of the queen's party and of the queen's cousin and most loyal supporter, Count Ulrich Cillei.[33] To justify the election of Wladislaus of Poland to the Hungarian throne, Thuróczy creates a Queen Elizabeth convinced of her own unsuitability for the task, in contradiction to Kottanner's depiction of her as well as other contemporary sources; it was a well-known fact that Emperor Sigmund had raised his daughter for the throne, to rule with her husband, and that Elizabeth was ambitious. Instead, Thuróczy has the queen hold the following (purely invented) speech: ". . . I am, as you know, the kingdom's heiress, but I do not think I am strong enough to guide the reins of the kingdom. If you are looking forward to the birth of my child, I believe I shall deliver a daughter rather than a son, to the extent that my woman's nature can know this from experience. Try, therefore, to find for yourself a prince who is more qualified than a woman to bear the responsibilities of so great a realm, keeping in your ears and before your eyes the kindnesses of my father, lest you arrange for me to have no share in the kingdom of him whose daughter I am." And the writer comments: "This speech of the queen kindled a great torch that

---

[31] See Pál Engel's foreword to Thuróczy's *Chronicle of the Hungarians*, 6; 14.
[32] Thuróczy, chap. 195, 30
[33] For example in chap. 229, 120–121.

blazed in Hungary for many years. For as a consequence of these words of the queen, the magnates themselves came to a unanimous agreement concerning the introduction of a new king."[34] A majority of Hungarian barons indeed agreed to the election of the Polish Wladislaus to the throne, but this had nothing to do with Elizabeth's alleged unwillingness or unsuitability for the regency. In keeping with this distortion of the facts, Thuróczy reports the election and official entrance into Hungary of Wladislaus III before he announces the birth and coronation of Ladislaus Posthumous, which makes the latter's coronation look like a silly, albeit moving, exercise.[35] The entire episode reflects Thuróczy's partisanship as well as the resentment of female rule which had a long tradition in Hungary.

Whereas Kottanner's account is practically devoid of physical description, as if she expected her audience to be familiar with the people and places mentioned, Thuróczy provides fairly detailed descriptions of physiognomy, usually at the end of a report of someone's death, describes castles, town walls, places, and locale, and lengthy battle scenes, usually military ventures against the Sultan. He must have taken this information from the narrative passages in the royal charters he consulted and included it no doubt because he was writing for posterity, an audience without personal knowledge of the events and personalities to be remembered.

Though not particularly learned or well-read, Thuróczy was not adverse to showing off a bit, obviously proud of what smatterings of classical learning he had been able to acquire. He refers to Alexander the Great and uses now and then a classical epithet or mythological allusion.[36] Perhaps this indicates that he was influenced, tangentially, by the emerging humanism of King Matthias' Renaissance court.

Thuróczy's attitude as a historian, at any rate, while still typically medieval when it comes to his overall philosophy of history, is also highly critical, and he refrains from moralizing, at least in this part of his *Chronicle*. He expresses his faith in divine providence and the providential plan that directs worldly affairs, but also repeatedly expresses cynicism with regard to the disorderly, often cruel, and seemingly senseless course of history.[37] His obvious political bias in addition to multiple errors of fact and inaccurate dating make him an unreliable source.

The Bavarian priest Jakob Unrest (c.1430–1500) is a more honest and faithful reporter. Like Helene Kottanner, he presents history from a

---

34 Thuróczy, chap. 223, 104–105.
35 See chaps. 223–224, 104–110.
36 References to "the driver of the Titan's chariot," chap. 248, 17; "the Fates," chap. 255, 195–196 and chap. 256, 201; etc.
37 For example: chap. 226, 114; chap. 229, 120; chap. 230, 123.

strictly medieval perspective according to which God, the Saints and the Devil interfere directly in life on earth. His *Hungarian Chronicle* gives a coherent history of Hungary from Attila to the rule of King Matthias Corvinus in the order of the successive kings. With the exception of the *Wiener Bilderchronik* by Heinrich von Mügeln, it is the first chronicle of Hungary written in German.[38] Unrest relied heavily on Thuróczy's Latin Chronicle but produced a free, personal rendition rather than a mere translation and included information from other sources, particularly Stainreuter. His *Austrian Chronicle* begins at the time of Elizabeth's father, Emperor Sigmund, and goes up to the end of the fifteenth century. Both chronicles report the untimely death of King Ladislaus (Posthumous) for whom Unrest had great hopes. It is to be noted that neither Thuróczy nor Unrest mention Kottanner, likely proof that her *Memoirs* reached only their intended audience and did not circulate among a wider readership; Thuróczy and Unrest, at any rate, did not know of her text or they would undoubtedly have used it.

Nevertheless, Unrest's text reads much like Kottanner's. The composition is continuous, without subdivision into paragraphs or chapters, and moves chronologically, while bringing together related events. There are often unsatisfactory transitions, the language and sentence structure are plain, and Unrest, like Kottanner, often resorts to stock phrases and set expressions, avoiding figures of speech or special effects of any kind. Unlike Kottanner, however, Unrest contradicts himself at times. His purpose in writing these chronicles was, as he said, to preserve worthy deeds, to honor the nobility, to edify the common man, and to understand the past, the present and the future.[39] His histories are traditional and patriarchal, barely reporting on Elizabeth or other female rulers.[40] As narratives, they lack the vividness and expressiveness that characterize Helene Kottanner's account.

But Queen Elizabeth's chambermaid, unlike János Thuróczy or Jakob Unrest, probably was not primarily writing for posterity. The German title of her text, bestowed by the nineteenth-century editors, is *Denkwürdigkeiten*, which in English means literally: "things worthy to be remembered." I do not know who first qualified Kottanner's recollections as "memoirs," but the term certainly comes closest to defining her text

---

[38] Jakob Unrest, *Österreichische Chronik*, ed. Karl Grossmann (Munich: Monumenta Germaniae Historica, 1957), repr. 1982, xvi.

[39] Ibid., xxvi

[40] A characteristic feature of medieval chronicles. The treatment of women in the tradition of narrative chronicles has not been studied much and deserves more attention. See *Medieval Women and the Sources of Medieval History*, ed. Joel T. Rosenthal (Athens: Univ. of Georgia Press, 1990), xiv.

from the point of view of genre. Whereas autobiography in a very general sense may be defined as "a retrospective account in prose that a real person makes of his own existence stressing his individual life and especially the history of his personality," memoirs are "usually written by public figures (ministers, military leaders, etc.) as soon as they have the leisure of retirement or exile and provide a sort of posthumous propaganda for posterity."[41] Memoirs usually celebrate the careers and views of famous men "who were never wrong," and therefore usually involve self-justification and self-glorification. As opposed to the inward gaze of autobiography, memoirs concentrate on the exterior aspects of a life and are presented to the reader "from the perspective of the time, so that their methodological problems are no different from those of the ordinary writing of history." In other words, while autobiography, more often than not, follows the subjective time of personal, inner experience and is therefore more akin to fiction, memoirs are generally considered to be more akin to historiography.[42] Yet one could argue that memoirs too are a form of self-revelation.

Just as the female autobiography may be quite distinct from the male tradition in autobiography, Helene Kottanner's *Memoirs* may not exactly fit the mold of traditional male memoirs.[43] In studying a great number of autobiographies by women writers from Margery Kempe to the twentieth century, Mary G. Mason found that "the self-discovery of female identity seems to acknowledge the real presence and recognition of another consciousness," so that "the disclosure of a female self is linked to the identification of some other."[44] Hence, it is, in Mason's view, women's interconnectedness with an other or others, be it in a state of dependency or on a basis of equality, that determines the very structure of female autobiography.[45] While this may not be the defining difference of women's autobiography, it is nevertheless interesting to keep in mind here, for Kottanner's early example of female memoirs is also structured around the narrator's relatedness with several significant others: Queen Elizabeth, her son, and God.

---

41 Clearly, this much quoted definition of autobiography by Philippe Lejeune (as translated by Olney, op. cit. 18) is not without problems but adequate for my purpose here, i.e. to show that the theoretical generic demarcations between autobiography and memoirs are superficial. The definition of memoirs is from Georges Gusdorf, "Conditions and Limits of Autobiography," in Olney, op. cit. 36.

42 Ibid., 36.

43 Mary G. Mason, "The Other Voice: Autobiographies of Women Writers," in Olney, 209–210. What exactly constitutes the "difference" of female autobiography is still not well understood.

44 Mary Mason, in Olney, 210.

45 See Domna Stanton's critique of Mason's theory in her introductory chapter to *The Female Autograph*, 12.

However, Kottanner's obtrusive, assertive female narrator is as unusual, in the context of late-medieval literature and historiography, as her preoccupation with a politically active and astute female monarch.[46] Traditional medieval historiographers, such as Jakob Unrest for example, typically ignore female royals or fail to take them seriously.

European Feudalism and the Position of Women
European feudalism was a political and military system designed to organize a society of which three percent were nobles and the rest peasants and to protect the West from military incursions from the North (Vikings), the East (Magyars) and the South (Saracens). It originated in central France in the early ninth century and gradually spread all over Europe. Based on the institutions of manorialism and serfdom, it was a system of mutual obligation whereby vassals swore loyalty to and performed military service for the lord, who in exchange provided military protection and local government. The lords in turn swore fealty to the prince or king.

The Hungarian feudal system resembled the French and German varieties, but the nobility, the peasants, and later the free cities had rights and obligations which showed local variations.[47] The Hungarian aristocrats were bound to their king not by feudal (vassalic) ties but by the fidelity due to the chief of an armed retinue by its members.[48] In the fifteenth century, the time recorded by Helene Kottanner, the Hungarian magnates, or barons, still completely dominated Hungarian politics and culture. They were the "great landowners whose power rested on extensive landed properties with several castles each and thousands of peasants." They were called "barons," not because they held baronial offices but because of their status and wealth.[49] As a separate group they were distinguished from the unfree commoners by their noble birth, their tenure as freeholders, and the privileged status such tenure conveyed. They were considered free men to whom even the king himself could not issue orders. In theory they were exempt from taxes, and had to go to war only in the rare instances when the country itself was attacked. Yet they had the right to intervene in political affairs and had a great deal of power.[50] From around 1440 onward, the major affairs of the kingdom were the

---

[46] See Ursula Liebertz-Grün, "Frau und Herrscherin," in *Auf der Suche nach der Frau im Mittelalter*, ed. Bea Lundt (Munich: Fink, 1991), 185.

[47] Peter Sugar, *A History of Hungary*, xi.

[48] Fügedi, 6: 8.

[49] János Bak, chap. 6 in *A History of Hungary*, eds. Sugar et al., 57.

[50] Pál Engel, foreword to Thuróczy's chronicle, 2–3.

responsibility of the Diet, a general assembly of nobility whose members either appeared personally or sent elected deputies to represent them.[51]

With respect to the problematic question of King Albert's succession, the Diet, composed of members of the county nobility hostile to Elizabeth, claimed its right to elect a king and chose Wladislaus of Poland, presumably on account of his military successes; the justification given was that they needed a king who could protect the country against the Ottoman invasions. However, an old and deep-rooted resentment against female rule may have had something to do with it as well. When Elizabeth upon Albert's death claimed the regency, the majority of Hungarian magnates refused to support her, regardless of whether the child would be male or female, because they did not want a long regency under a woman.[52]

The feudal system being in the first place a military system whose hierarchical structure was defined by the composing members' ability to contribute soldiers for warfare and perform in battle, women were never fully part of it, although early on the succession of females to fiefs was possible. Yet women were allowed to inherit fiefs only on the condition that the lord reserved the right to choose the woman's husband who then had to assume vassal's responsibilities, i.e. military service to the lord.[53] "The rulers of post-Carolingian Europe personally embodied public power and earned their legitimacy in part through the religious authority they bore. Initially, their wives, as property owners in their own right and controllers of land held in fief, shared this authority." But after the twelfth century, as recent research has indicated, changes in the nature of the state and in the idea of rule undermined the power of the woman consort.[54]

A German chronicler like Ottokar von Steiermark gives a good idea of the prevailing view of female rulers. In his *Steirischen Reimchronik*, which traces the "history of the world" from the death of Emperor Frederick II (1250) to the South-Austrian revolt against the Habsburg ruler Duke Frederick I (1309), he shows that women's right to inherit and hold property frequently led to political quarrels. More often than not, one cannot help but wonder whether these women served any other purpose but to function as a vehicle to transfer titles from one man to

---

[51] Idem.

[52] Macartney, op. cit. 51–52.

[53] David Herlihy, *The History of Feudalism* (New York: Harper & Row, 1970), 77. See also F. L. Ganshof, *Feudalism* (New York: Harper & Row, 1961), 143–144.

[54] Martha Howell, Suzanne Wemple and Denise Kaiser, "A Documented Presence: Medieval Women in Germanic Historiography," in *Women in Medieval History and Historiography*, ed. Susan Mosher Stuard (Philadelphia: Univ. of Pennsylvania Press, 1987), 114.

another. Frequently, even the privilege of female succession did not guarantee them a position of power.[55]

In Hungary, female succession was always problematic. It had led to civil war even in recent memory, when Louis the Great, the last Angevin King of Hungary and Poland, died in 1382. He was succeeded by the eldest of his two young daughters, the eleven-year-old Mary, under the regency of her mother, Elizabeth. However, their succession was opposed by the great lords of the Southeast, by the Horváti clan, and by a great many lesser nobles "who found the inheritance in female line an anomaly."[56] They rose in open revolt and invited the last male representative of the House of Anjou to the Hungarian throne. Thus, Charles II was crowned king on 31 December 1385. But the queens fought back, and thirty-nine days after his coronation, Charles was assassinated by their agents. Nevertheless, the queens were eventually forced to accept defeat. Elizabeth was strangled and her daughter Mary married off to Sigmund, who was crowned King of Hungary in March 1387.[57]

Similarly, in the case described by Kottanner, the Hungarian barons preferred the sixteen-year-old male Wladislaus of Poland (not a relative, but the barons advanced the long standing friendship between Hungary and Poland as a comparable tie) to the regency of Albert's thirty-one-year-old widow Elizabeth, only daughter of Emperor Sigmund who had raised her for the throne. Contrary to her father's intentions, however, Elizabeth received no share in the affairs of the government, and her own coronation was performed with a lesser crown and not by the Archbishop of Esztergóm, as were those of Albert and later the little Ladislaus, but by a lesser prelate, the Bishop of Veszprém.[58] Yet, after Albert's death, Elizabeth never once considered renouncing the throne. Although she consented to inviting the Polish Wladislaus to Hungary, this was mostly a ruse to keep the dissenting Hungarian nobles at bay and to buy time while she awaited the birth of the baby.

The tradition of misogyny that thwarted the political aspirations of Queen Elizabeth and the Hungarian queens before her persisted long after her death, unaffected by the Renaissance or humanism. In the century following that of Helene Kottanner, "women, especially noblewomen, were reckoned as and had to consider themselves tools to be used for dynastic purposes. They had to be ready to sacrifice their own needs and desires in order to serve effectively as vessels carrying and agents

---

[55] Liebertz-Grün, "Frau und Herrscherin," 81.
[56] Janos Bak in *A History of Hungary*, ed. Peter Sugar et al., 54–55.
[57] This Mary was the first wife of Sigmund of Luxembourg. The mother of Queen Elizabeth was his second wife, Barbara Cillei.
[58] János Bak, *Königtum und Stände*, Appendix 2: 169.

securing the inheritance of their family, the means by which position was preserved, fortunes acquired, maintained, and enlarged."[59] Female monarchs were not taken seriously as rulers. Thus it was that John Henckel, a preacher at her court in Hungary, could say of Mary of Habsburg (1505–1558), who was briefly Queen of Hungary and later regent of the Netherlands: "If only she could be changed into a king our affairs would be in better shape."[60]

The situation changed somewhat when Emperor Charles VI, by means of the Pragmatic Sanction of 1720, modified the succession laws in the Austrian domains to make his daughters, the eldest of whom was Maria Theresa, successors to the throne. However, that decision was inspired mostly by Charles' desire that the Austrian Empire should remain undivided. For the same reason, the Sanction also stipulated that in case of the extinction of Charles' line, the daughters of Joseph I and their descendants were to inherit the lands belonging to the Austrian Empire. This Pragmatic Sanction was accepted by the Hungarian Diet in 1723, and Maria Theresa became Queen of Hungary and Archduchess of Austria upon her father's death in 1740.

The Holy Crown of Hungary

In Hungary, an elected king was not considered a legal ruler of that country until he had been inaugurated with the Holy Crown.[61] This Holy Crown of St. Stephen was considered to have been sent, in the year 1000, by Pope Sylvester II to St. Stephen (Istvan), king and patron saint of Hungary from 997 to 1038. It is still in existence. Although experts who have examined the crown differ much on its origin and date, most agree that no part of it can go back to the eleventh century. Nevertheless, ascribed to St. Stephen, it has been considered a sacred symbol of the Hungarian nation ever since the middle of the thirteenth century, and without it no elected Hungarian king, no matter how great his support, could effectively assume governmental power.[62] This is the reason why the Polish Wladislaus, although he had the support of the majority of the Hungarian county nobility and although all the other royal paraphernalia were used at this coronation on 17 July 1440, was not considered a truly legitimate king. This is the reason why Queen Elizabeth devised her secret stratagem and why her confidante Helene Kottanner got involved in

59 David P. Daniel, "Piety, Politics, and Perversion: Noblewomen in Reformation Hungary," in *Women in Reformation and Counter-Reformation Europe*, ed. Sherrin Marshall (Bloomington: Indiana Univ. Press, 1989), 69.
60 Ibid., 70; 86, n. 3.
61 See Fügedi, 1: 179.
62 Ibid., 1: 181.

affairs of state at the highest level. And this is also why Helene Kottanner's *Memoirs* are so significant; here are two late-medieval women who not only shape the most important political events of their day but also manipulate the very symbol of political power in Hungary.

The Text
Kottanner's graphic descriptions and her conscious preparation and development of culminating points in the narrative reveal the skill of an expert stylist and master of composition. Structurally, the *Memoirs* consist of five chronologically ordered and thematically focused blocks that flow logically one out of the other and build up to a climax, then follow a descending line. The opening section, a summary of the preceding events, leads up to King Albert's sudden death which leaves Elizabeth a widow responsible for her children's future. The second part concentrates on the theft of the Holy Crown and ends with Ladislaus' birth and baptism. The atmosphere of fear and foreboding expressed in the impressionistic evocation of evil forces operative during the night of the theft contrasts sharply with the mood of triumph pervading the description of the coronation in the third, climactic, part. The flight of the royal family to Raab marks a reversal of fortune that seems complete when all have to go their separate ways in the last part. The journey from the coronation city Stuhlweissenburg to Raab took only two or three days but as presented by Helene Kottanner it seems to last much longer. Her dramatic portrayal of this exodus beset by dangers and curiously extreme and constantly changing weather conditions leaves a lasting impression of mental anguish and physical suffering borne bravely for a crown and all that it stood for.

The Memoirs of Helene Kottanner (1439–1440)

1. When after the birth of Christ fourteen hundred years had passed, and when after that the thirty-ninth year had advanced to Easter [5 April 1439] and to Pentecost [24 May 1439], and when the noble King Albert had been elected Holy Roman King and then had received the crown of Hungary, and the queen had received it too, his grace came to Pressburg and did not stay here long.[1] Then the noble queen, the Lady Elizabeth, left Ofen in order to join her husband and came to Pressburg.[2] Then King Albert came from Austria to Pressburg with his court.[3] And then his grace sent a delegation to Vienna to fetch and bring to him in Pressburg his youngest daughter, Princess Elizabeth, with all her servants.[4] And that happened. And I, Helene Kottanner, was there too, for I had been sent along to the court of King Albert and also of his wife, the noble and most gracious queen.

Not long thereafter, we left with the queen and the noble young princess and rode off to Ofen. We had not been in Ofen very long when there was an uprising against the Germans.[5] And then the Bishop of Gran, whose name was George Pelóczi, died.[6] Since the Holy Crown was in Gran at that time, King Albert went to the Lords Pelóczi, brothers of the bishop, who were then in charge of Gran.[7] And King Albert found that the Holy Crown as well as the paraments were safely in their place. Then the lords named Pelóczi deliberated among themselves and sent a messenger to the Church Council at the castle at Gran, and there too were

---

1 Duke Albert V of Austria, b. 1397, married King Sigmund's daughter Elizabeth in 1422. They were crowned sovereigns of Hungary in the coronation city Stuhlweissenburg (Székesfehérvár) on 1 January 1438. Albert was elected Roman King (Albert II) on 18 March 1438. Pressburg is the present city of Bratislava.
2 Ofen (Hung. Buda) on the Danube is now the eastern part of the Hungarian capital.
3 Albert was in Vienna from 8 April to 20 April 1439.
4 Princess Elizabeth was born in 1436, hence three years old at this point in the narrative.
5 There was a plebeian revolt against the German merchants in Buda on 23 May 1439.
6 Gran, northwest of Budapest on the Danube, is now Esztergóm. George Pelóczi, Archbishop of Gran since 1432, had crowned King Albert on 1 January 1438, and since the coronation kept the royal crowns and insignia in his castle at Gran. The queen was crowned by the Bishop of Wesprim (Hung. Veszprém) with a lesser crown.
7 Simon and Ladislaus Pelóczi were actually nephews of the Archbishop. On the Holy Crown, see introduction 18–19.

many meetings.[8] Then it became clear that they did not support King Albert of the Holy Crown but that they were opposed to the king.[9] But listen now to what happened in the meantime; the queen, Lady Elizabeth, had become pregnant. And later she bore King Albert a noble son, whose name was Lászlá.[10]

When the deliberations about the Holy Crown had come to an end, the noble King Albert sent his youngest daughter, the noble princess, Lady Elizabeth, to the stronghold at Plintenburg, and I, Helene Kottanner, went along too.[11] And still on the same day, the noble King Albert and his wife, the noble queen, rode off to Gran to claim the Holy Crown, which was given to them. Then his grace went off to address his soldiers in Szegedin.[12] And when he was ready to depart, he immediately went to Plintenburg with his wife, the noble queen, and carried with him the Holy Crown to his youngest daughter, the princess.

A number of Hungarian nobles accompanied them, and together they carried the Holy Crown and brought it into a pentagonal vault.[13] And I, Helene Kottanner, was there too, carrying the young princess on my arm, and I saw clearly how they placed the Holy Crown there. Then they closed the vault and covered the door to the vault with many seals. Plintenburg was at that time in the hands of the noble lords Count Nicholas of Posing and his son George.

Then the noble King Albert and his wife, the noble queen, rode off again to the king's army and the unrest near Szegedin. And what happened after that is well known; not long afterwards the noble king became sick with the illness called dysentery. And the steward of the royal household ordered that the ailing king be taken back to Plintenburg, where they laid him down in the lower castle.[14]

Then the king's physicians from Vienna came to see him, and when his grace had improved a little, his young daughter, the princess, sent him a little shift which belonged to her and which she had worn on her own body.[15] Then his grace sent the little gown back to the queen's castle to a

8   After the death of the archbishop, the administration of the Church was taken over by the Church Council until a new archbishop had been elected.
9   Many Hungarian nobles, including the lords Pelóczi, wanted to limit the king's power in favor of their own territorial ambitions.
10 Ladislaus Posthumous, b.21 February 1440.
11 The Plintenburg stronghold (Visegrád) was north of Budapest.
12 Hung. Szeged, in south Hungary. Albert had to address his soldiers on account of threats from the Turkish side.
13 The king's treasury on the ground floor. Cf. Mollay, 18.
14 The king's castle was at the foot of the citadel, the queen's residence in the upper part of the stronghold.
15 It was believed that illnesses both in humans and in animals could be cured or even prevented by wiping or rubbing the body with a shift. Cf. Mollay, 51.

loyal servant, a pious man named Vinsterel, and had him make a little pouch out of it with a brooch and two amulets with magic pea-pods.[16] After that, the queen rode off to the estate of Lord Ladislaus Garai, the Ban, in Ofen, and her heart was heavy, because the noble King Albert had wanted her to stay with him.[17] He sent her many messages, particularly when the queen would not return to him, and he urged her to come to him just once before he would depart from there.[18] That would have been in the interest of both. Then his grace left Plintenburg although he was still ill. He still wanted to see his young daughter, Princess Elizabeth, and then his grace rode off to Gran. But in Langendorf his illness got worse, and then the noble king and sovereign, Albert, died, on the day before the feast of the blessed Apostles Simon and Jude [27 October 1439].[19]

2. That same morning, an Hungarian lord named . . . came to see the young princess at Plintenburg who said that he wanted to speak immediately to the noble queen, her mother.[20] And he refused to go away, and they eventually listened to him, which was wise. He spoke with our gracious lady and told her that the noble King Albert had removed the Holy Crown from Plintenburg and taken it away from there. This frightened her grace at once. Then her grace wrote to Count Nicholas of Posing and to Count George, his son.[21] She wanted to know whether this news was true or not and that they should inform her about this. Then the two counts I just mentioned came to me and talked to me in secret, and together we went to the door which gave access to the Holy Crown. But all the seals were still whole and intact, and so they wrote to the noble queen to this effect.

But then her grace wanted to find out the truth for herself, and she came to Plintenburg with many Hungarian magnates, and they all went into the vault and carried the trunk with the Holy Crown out of the vault and then took the Holy Crown and its casing, which was covered with many seals, out of the trunk. They broke the seals and took the Holy Crown out of the box and examined it very carefully. And I was there too. Then they took the Holy Crown and placed it into a smaller box which also contained the

---

16 Both in German and in Hungarian folk medicine, pea-pods are known to prevent disease as well as magic spells.

17 Banus or Ban designates a high administrative function in medieval Hungary. Ladislaus Garai was Ban of Matschovia, an area between Bosnia and Serbia.

18 King Albert was suspicious of his ambitious wife, who as only daughter of King Sigmund claimed ever more influence. He himself wanted to go to Vienna to regain his strength, as his physicians had probably advised him.

19 Langendorf (Hung. Neszmély): approx. 30 km. from Gran and 50 km. from Plintenburg.

20 The identity of this Hungarian nobleman remains unknown.

21 Castellans of the Plintenburg stronghold.

other crown, the one which had been used for the noble queen's coronation as queen of Hungary.[22]

The two crowns stood side by side in one box, and near the box stood a bed, and here the noble queen lay down to rest with her heavy burden. Sleeping in the same room with her were two ladies-in-waiting; one was called Barbara, the daughter of an Hungarian nobleman, and the name of the other was Lady Frodnach. Near them stood a wax candle as a light for the night, as is the custom with noble ladies. Then it happened that one of the ladies-in waiting got up during the night and did not notice that the candle fell over and caused a fire in the room which reached the box with the two crowns in it and singed it and also burnt a hole bigger than a fist in the blue velvet pillow lying on top of the box. And now take note of the miracle! The king who was to wear the Holy Crown was still safely enclosed in his mother's body and he and the crown, which the evil fiend would have liked to destroy with the fire, were hardly two cords removed from one another, but God watched over us and awakened the ladies in time, while I slept in the front room with the little princess. Then these ladies came to me and told me to get up at once because there was a fire in my gracious lady's bedroom. Terrified, I arose immediately and rushed to the room which was full of smoke, and I tempered the fire and extinguished it and let the smoke out and made the room clean and safe again, so that the noble queen was able to sleep there quietly that night.

The following morning, the Hungarian lords came to see my gracious lady, and her grace told them what had happened to her during the night and how she and the Holy Crown as well as the other crown had almost perished in the fire. The lords marveled at this and recommended that the Holy Crown be placed into the trunk again and returned to the vault where it had been before. That was done the same day. And they pressed seals on the door, as before, although there were not as many seals as had been there previously.

When that had been done, my gracious lady sent a messenger to Count George of Posing, asking him to give her the keys to Plintenburg because the Hungarian magnates wanted her to entrust the stronghold to the care of Ladislaus Garai, her cousin. And this happened. And Lord Ladislaus Garai, the Ban, took charge of the castle and administered it together with a castellan.

Then, as the noble queen readied herself to return to Ofen with her cousin Ladislaus and the other Hungarian magnates, she secretly confided in me and said: "Dear, faithful mother Kottanner, watch over my daughter and also over that room. Do not allow anyone to enter it except my

22 See 21, n. 6.

daughter and yourself." She also entrusted to me for safekeeping her own crown and her necklace and other jewels, all of which I kept in the room through which one had to pass to get to the Holy Crown. And as we were speaking with one another like this, Lord Ladislaus joined us with his castellan and said: "Gracious lady, give this woman orders not to allow anyone into that room, not even my castellan." But her grace responded wisely and said to me: "Dear Helene Kottanner, when my cousin, Lord Ladislaus, and his castellan want to go inside, let them go in." Then the castellan went to the door with the seals on it and took a small piece of cloth and placed it over the seals and tied it into a knot and then pressed his own seal on it.

When all this had happened, the noble widow, my gracious lady, rode off to Ofen with her cousin, Lord Ladislaus, and with the other Hungarian nobles. And she was burdened with many problems and beset by many worries, because the Hungarian magnates wanted her to take a husband and had already proposed to her several candidates, one of whom was the King of Poland named Wladislaus, another the son of the Serbian despot.[23]

The queen was deeply troubled by all this, but she gave them many courteous answers and said: "Dear lords, please do not give me a pagan; I would sooner marry a Christian peasant." Then her cousin Lord Ladislaus resolved that she should take the Polish king. And then all the Hungarian lords insisted that she do that. But she did not want to and answered them that she wanted to wait and see what God would give her and that she would decide accordingly, for all her physicians had told her that she was carrying a son, and that was what she was hoping for. But as she could not know the truth yet and could not use it to determine a course of action, her grace left Ofen again and rode back to Plintenburg and moved into the king's quarters below. And Count Ulrich Cillei joined her there.[24]

When the Hungarian lords learned this, they soon came to her grace and pressed the case of the King of Poland. Then someone advised her to feign her willingness to marry the Polish king, while pursuing in the meantime whatever would be best for her, and they would always be able to find a reason to get out of her promise. Her grace did this and pretended that she was prepared to take the Polish king as her husband. However,

---

[23] Wladislaus III of Poland, b. 1424. Though crowned king immediately after the death of his father in May 1434, he was given the power to rule only in 1439. He was at most sixteen years old. The other candidate was Lazarus, the youngest son of the Despot George Brancoviç of Serbia (1427–1456).

[24] Ulrich Cillei (1406–1456), cousin of both Queen Elizabeth and Ladislaus Garai, unlike Garai, was always on Queen Elizabeth's side.

she stated three conditions, which are well known.[25] She said that if they could fulfill them, she would marry the King of Poland. But she knew full well that none of them, neither the King of Poland nor the Hungarian magnates, could satisfy the three conditions, and in this manner she intended to get out of the promise she had made to marry the Polish king. The magnates did not see through this and were happy that she had accepted to wed the Polish king.

Since the wise and noble queen understood this, she thought for a long time about possible ways to get the Holy Crown in her possession, away from the Hungarian lords. She thought namely that if she were to be delivered of a son, he should not be ousted from his realm, and that if she were to be delivered of a daughter, she might still be able to negotiate with the Hungarian magnates and obtain concessions from them. She therefore asked me, already then, if I would be prepared to go and fetch the Holy Crown, although the right time had not come yet. As you will hear henceforth, however, it was truly a mistake to think that the right time had not yet come for God Almighty to perform His miraculous deeds.

The Hungarian magnates would have preferred it if her grace had stayed at Plintenburg to deliver the child, but the idea did not please her grace at all and she did not do it and also refused to move into her own castle at the top of the fortress. With her great wisdom she feared that if she went up there, she and the child could be kept there by force. The other reason was that they would be less inclined to suspect that she was after the Holy Crown. Then the noble queen brought her youngest daughter, Princess Elizabeth, from the upper castle down to the palace below, and also summoned me as well as two ladies-in-waiting to accompany her and left the others up there, including a duchess from Silezia and other noble ladies. All the people wondered why her grace had left these ladies-in-waiting and the other servants of my young mistress up there. And why that was, nobody knows but God except her grace and myself.

And I had the keys to the room where her crown, her necklace and her other jewels were kept. Then, all of a sudden, her grace had to go to the countryside in secret and ordered me to go to the castle above to try and secretly bring her crown and jewelry down to the castle below. I did this and went to the queen's residence above and in utmost secrecy brought down from there my gracious lady's crown and all her jewelry on a sled, hiding everything under my clothes. And as I entered the courtyard of the lower castle, some Hungarian lords rode up to meet me, and Lord

---

[25] I haven't been able to find anywhere what exactly these three conditions were.

Ladislaus Garai asked me: "Helene Kottanner, what is it you are bringing with you?" – "I am bringing my clothes."

My gracious lady was happy that I had brought her the jewelry, and now I had to keep the crown in the room where my young mistress and I slept, because there were very few rooms there which could be locked. And I kept it under the bed and worried much about it, because we did not have any trunks there. If the lords had seen the box with the crown, they would have mistaken it for the Holy Crown, which would have caused a lot of trouble and talk, and they also would have understood why her grace had had to leave on a secret journey through the country.

When the noble queen had answered the Hungarian lords concerning the matter with the Polish king in the manner you have heard, and when the letter and the Hungarian nobles who would take it to the Polish king – the Bishop of Erlau, Lord Matko, Imre Marcali, and other magnates – were ready, these Hungarian lords left Plintenburg and went off to Ofen. Then the noble queen left the stronghold too and went with her little daughter, the Lady Elizabeth, to Komorn.[26] Count Ulrich Cillei, her loyal friend, joined her there, and they deliberated with one another and together devised a way to get the Holy Crown out of the Plintenburg stronghold.

Then my gracious lady came to me and said that I should do it because there was no one she could trust who knew the place as well as I did. The queen's request frightened me, for it meant great danger for me and my little children. And I weighed the matter in my mind, wondering what to do, and there was no one I could ask for advice except God alone. I said to myself that if I did not do it and something evil happened as a result, then I would have sinned against God and the world. And so I said that I was willing to undertake that difficult journey even at the risk of losing my life, but I asked that they give me a helper. They asked my advice as to who I thought would be suitable for that, and I recommended a man who I thought was wholly loyal and devoted to my lady, and this man was from Croatia. They called him in and informed him of our secret plan and proposed what they wanted from him. But the man was so overcome by fear that all the color drained from his face as if he were half dead, and he did not agree to co-operate but instead went out to his horses in the stable. I do not know whether it was the will of God or whether this man was careless at other times as well, but soon the news reached us from the lower castle that he had made a very bad fall from his horse. And when his condition had improved, he mounted his horse and rode off to Croatia, so that we had to postpone our plan.

---

[26] Komorn (Hung. Komárom) on the Danube is about 65 km. west of Plintenburg.

It saddened my gracious lady that the coward knew about this business, and I too was deeply concerned, but it all truly was the will of God. For if we had carried out our plan at that very time, my gracious lady still would have been pregnant while traveling to Pressburg with the Holy Crown, and then the noble child she still carried in her body might not have been crowned king, for she probably would not have had the assistance and power then which she had later, as it has turned out.

But when the time had come when the Almighty God wished to perform His miraculous deeds, God sent us a man who was willing to abduct the Holy Crown. He was Hungarian, and his name was . . .[27] He was loyal and wise and sensible in the way he took care of this business. We prepared the things we needed for the undertaking and took several locks and two files. And he who was to risk his life with me donned a black velvet night shift and two felt shoes, and in each shoe he placed a file and he hid the locks underneath his shirt. And I took my gracious lady's small signet, and I also took the keys to the first door; for there were three of them, because near the door-hinge there was another chain and a bolt, where before our departure from the stronghold we had attached another lock to prevent that anyone else would affix one there. And when we were ready to go, my lady first sent a messenger ahead of us to Plintenburg to inform the castellan and the lords in charge of the ladies-in-waiting, Franz of Pöker and Ladislaus Tamási, that the ladies should pack and be ready for the carriage that would come to take them to my lady's castle in Komorn, for she had had to go to Pressburg.[28] This was announced to all the members of the queen's household. Then, when the carriage destined for the ladies-in-waiting was ready, and the sled in which I and he who shared my concerns were to travel was ready as well, they sent us two Hungarian noblemen to accompany me to the ladies-in-waiting. Then we set out on our journey.

When the castellan learned the news that I was coming to fetch the ladies-in-waiting, it surprised him and all the other members of the queen's court as well that they had allowed me to go so far away from my young mistress who was still young and who did not like me to leave her, as they all knew very well. Then it happened that the castellan felt a bit ill and would have liked to place his bed near the door that formed the first entrance to the Holy Crown. But then his illness worsened, which was the will of God, and because that door was in the room of the women, he was reluctant to allow his servants to sleep there with him. So then he

---

[27] We possess no sure information concerning the identity of this collaborator.
[28] Where she wanted to await the birth of the child.

wrapped a small piece of linen cloth around the lock which we had placed near the door-hinge and pressed his seal on it.

When we arrived at Plintenburg, the ladies-in-waiting were cheerful and looked forward to their trip to my noble mistress, and they were getting themselves ready and had ordered a trunk to be made for their wardrobe. We had to wait for a long time, and the hammering went on until after 8 o'clock. To while away the time, my companion joined us in the room and conversed with the ladies. In front of the stove, there lay some firewood which was used to heat it, and he hid the files underneath this wood. But some servants of the ladies-in-waiting happened to see the files underneath the wood and began to whisper among themselves. I overheard them and immediately told him about it. My words frightened him so much that all color drained from his face, and he quickly retrieved the files and hid them somewhere else.

And he said to me: "Woman, see to it that we have light." So I asked an old woman to give me some candles, explaining that I had to say many prayers because it was Saturday night [20 February 1440], the first Saturday after Ash Wednesday. I took the candles and concealed them carefully. And when all the ladies-in-waiting and everybody else had gone to sleep, I remained in the little room with an old woman I had brought with me who did not know a word of German and who also knew nothing of our plan and was unfamiliar with the castle. She lay there and was fast asleep.

When it was time, he who shared my burden came through the chapel and knocked on the door. I let him in and locked the door again behind him. To assist him with the work, he had brought along a man, whose Christian name was . . ., the same as his, who had sworn loyalty to him. I go to them and want to bring them the candles, but the candles were gone.[29] I became so afraid that I did not know any more what to do, and the whole undertaking almost failed only because we had no light. Then I came to my senses and went and secretly awakened the woman who had given me the candles, and I told her that the candles were gone and that I still had much praying to do. To my great relief she gave me others which I gave to him, and I also gave him the locks to attach there later, and I also gave him my gracious lady's small signet with which he was to replace the seals, and I also gave him the three keys to the first door.[30]

Then he removed from the lock the linen cloth which the castellan had wrapped around it and unlocked the door and went inside with his servant,

---

[29] Here the narrator suddenly slips twice into present tense, as if she were truly reliving that moment of extreme anxiety.

[30] Adjoining the treasure vault.

and they worked so hard on the other locks, that the sounds of their hammering and filing could be heard distinctly. But even if the guards and the castellan's men had been on the alert that night and actively watching the treasure entrusted to their care, then surely God Almighty would have stopped their ears to prevent them from hearing anything. But I alone heard everything very well and kept watch while invaded by many fears and worries, and I kneeled down in deep devotion and prayed to God and to Our Dear Lady, that they might assist me and my helpers. Yet I feared more for my soul than for my life, and I begged God that if the undertaking were against His will, I should be damned for it; or if something evil should result for the country and the people, that God have mercy on my soul and let me die here on the spot.

As I was praying like this, I suddenly heard loud noises and a rumble, as if there were a great many armored men at the door through which I had admitted my helper, and I had the impression that they were about to force open the door. This frightened me and I stood up, wanting to warn them to stop the work. But then it occurred to me that I should go to the door first, and I did. But when I reached the door, the noises were gone and I did not hear anybody any more. Then I said to myself that it must have been a ghost, and I resumed my prayers and promised Our Dear Lady to make a pilgrimage, barefoot, to Zell and vowed that as long as I had not performed the pilgrimage I would not sleep on feathers on Saturday nights.[31] And on every Saturday night as long as I live I also say a special prayer to Our Dear lady, to thank her for the mercy she has bestowed on me. And I beg her to thank for me her Son, Our Dear Lord Jesus Christ, for the great mercy and compassion he has so clearly manifested toward me.

But while I was praying like this, I seemed to hear loud noises and the din of armor at the door that led directly into the apartment of the ladies-in-waiting.[32] This frightened me so much that my entire body began to shake with fear and I broke into a cold sweat, and I thought that it must not be a ghost after all and that while I stood at the chapel door, they had gone around to the other side; and I did not know what to do and strained my ears to see if I could hear the ladies. But I did not hear anyone. Then I went softly down the steps through the room of the little princess to the door that led directly to the room of the ladies. And when I arrived at that door, I heard no one. Then I was relieved and thanked God and

---

[31] Mariazell in Steiermark was a popular pilgrimage place. To atone for her sins, Helene Kottanner promises to sleep on straw, or perhaps plain wood, instead of feathers, on Saturday nights.

[32] Namely, the entrance from the courtyard.

resumed my prayers once more and said to myself that it surely was the Devil, who would have liked to foil our plan.

When I had said all my prayers, I stood up and wanted to go into the vault to see what they were doing. Then he came to meet me and said that I could be pleased, because everything had gone well; they had filed the locks off the door, but the locks on the crown's casing were so tight that they had been unable to file them off and had had to burn them open. There was so much smoke that I worried that some people might ask about it, but God prevented that.

When the Holy Crown was completely free, we again closed the doors everywhere, replaced the locks that they had removed, pressed my lady's seals on them once more, and locked the outer door again and tied the piece of cloth with the seal on it as we had found it and as the castellan had put it there. And I threw the files in the privy in the room of the ladies, where you will find them, if you break it open, as proof that I am speaking the truth.

We carried the Holy Crown through the chapel of Saint Elizabeth, to which I, Helene Kottanner, still owe a chasuble and an altar cloth to be paid for by my gracious lord, King Ladislaus.[33] Then my helper took a red velvet pillow, opened it, removed part of the feathers, put the Holy Crown into the pillow, and sewed it back up. It was now almost day, and the ladies-in-waiting and everybody else were getting up and readying themselves for the journey thence.

Now the ladies-in-waiting had in their service an old woman who worked for them, and my gracious lady had given orders to give this woman her pay and then leave her behind, so she could return home to Ofen. But when the woman had been paid, she came to me, saying that she had seen something unusual lying in front of the stove and did not know what it was. This worried me, for I realized that it was part of the casing in which the crown had stood, and I talked the idea out of her head as well as I could, and then I went secretly to the stove and threw into the fire whatever remnants I could find and burned them completely. And I took the old woman along with me on the journey. They all wondered why I did this. I told them that I had taken it upon myself to try and obtain from the queen a position for her at St. Martin's in Vienna, as indeed I did.

When the queen's ladies and her entire retinue were ready to ride off, he who shared my anxiety took the pillow with the Holy Crown sewn

---

[33] This is a direct appeal to King Ladislaus to settle his, and his mother's, debts to Kottanner. Elizabeth of Thüringen (1207–1231), daughter of King Andrew II of Hungary. She was canonized in 1235. Until 1539 her remains were in Marburg-an-der Lahn. What the reliquary in the Plintenburg chapel contained is unknown. Cf. Mollay, 55 n. 68.

inside it and ordered his helper to carry the pillow out of the castle onto the sled in which he and I were to sit. So then the good fellow took the pillow on his shoulders and put over it an old cowhide with a long tail which dangled behind him. And all the people followed him with their eyes and began to laugh. When we had come down from the castle and reached the market, we would have liked to eat, but all we could find was herring, so we ate a little of that. And when we finished singing the mass, the hour was already far advanced, and we still had to travel from Plintenburg to Komorn that day, which we did, even though this is a distance of twelve miles. When we were about to ride off and taking our seats, I quickly felt over the pillow to know where the Holy Crown was so I would not sit down on it. And I thanked God Almighty for His mercy, although I kept looking back frequently for fear that anyone might be following us. Indeed, I worried incessantly, and thoughts were crowding in my mind, and I marveled at what God had done or might still do.

During my stay at the castle, I had not had a single peaceful night because of the important task entrusted to me, and I had many bad dreams. One night in particular, I dreamed that a woman had penetrated through the wall into the vault and carried off the Holy Crown. I was terrified and got up right away and took a maid of honor, whose name is Dachpeck, with me to the vault. But there I found everything as I had left it. The Lady Dachpeck then said to me: "It is no wonder that you cannot sleep well; great things have been entrusted to you." Thereupon we went back to our beds. And about all this I was thinking during the journey.[34]

When we had reached the inn where we intended to eat, the good fellow took the pillow of which he was in charge, followed me carrying it to the place where we wanted to eat, and laid it down across from me, so that I could watch it while we were eating. After the meal, the good fellow took the pillow and put it on the sled again as before, and so we rode off and traveled until the darkness of night.

Then we reached the Danube, which was still covered with ice, but the ice had gotten thin in several places. When we were on the ice and had come as far as the middle of the Danube, the carriage of the ladies-in-waiting proved too heavy; the ice broke and the carriage toppled over, the ladies screamed, and there was much chaos and confusion. I was afraid and thought that we and the Holy Crown would all perish in the Danube together. Yet God came to our rescue. None of our people went under, but of the things that were on the carriage several fell into the water and disappeared underneath the ice. Then I took the duchess from Silezia and

---

[34] The passage is unclear; from the foregoing one would conclude that Kottanner spent just one night at the Plintenburg stronghold before returning to the queen with the Holy Crown.

the highest-ranking ladies into my sled, and with the help of God we made it safely across the ice, and all the others did too.

When we arrived at the queen's castle in Komorn, he who shared my anxiety took the pillow with the Holy Crown and carried it inside to a place where it would be safe. And when I arrived in the ladies' quarters to see my gracious lady, I was received immediately by the noble queen who now knew well that with the help of God I had been a good messenger. But of the wondrous and truly miraculous assistance of God which had manifested itself there, her grace knows nothing, and she died before she had the opportunity to learn of it.[35] It was never possible for me to be alone with her long enough to tell her the entire story from beginning to end, for we were not together much longer.[36] And I also never had the opportunity to ask the one who shared my secret whether while working in the vault he had experienced the same miracle as I had witnessed, for he did not know much German and there was no one I could trust who could have translated for me.

The queen was lying on her bed resting a little when she received me, and she told me the events of the day. Two honorable ladies, both widows, had come to her grace from Ofen. One was called Lady Siebenlinder, the name of the other was Lady Zauzach. They had brought with them two nurses; one was a mid-wife, the other a wet-nurse to suckle the baby with her own breasts. And this wet-nurse had brought along her own child, a boy, for the wise say that the milk of a woman who has given birth to a son is better than the milk of a woman who has brought forth a daughter.[37] These women were to have accompanied the queen to Pressburg to assist her with the delivery there, for according to the calculations her grace was to carry the child for another week. It may be that the calculations were wrong, or that God willed otherwise; at any rate, if the queen had not gone into labor that night, her grace would have left early the next morning, for all the carriages were packed and the royal court was ready to depart.

As I was talking to the noble queen like this, her grace told me that the women from Ofen had bathed her in a tub and that after the bath she had felt quite unwell. Hence I lifted up her gown to see her naked. Then I saw several signs that showed me clearly that the birth of the child was not far off. By now, the ladies from Ofen were in their lodgings on the other side of the market. But we had another mid-wife with us, whose name was

---

[35] Queen Elizabeth died on 17 December 1442, only 4 days after a preliminary peace treaty with the Polish Wladislaus promised to end the civil war.

[36] Shortly after the coronation the members of the royal family went their separate ways for safety reasons; since Helene Kottanner was designated to take care of the little king, she had to take leave of the queen. They apparently never saw each other again.

[37] This discriminatory view was widely held in Antiquity and the Middle Ages.

Margret and who had been sent to my grace by the wife of Count Hanns of Schaunberg. She was supposed to be very good, which turned out to be true. Then I said: "Gracious lady, get up; it seems to me you will not go to Pressburg tomorrow."

Then her grace got up from the bed and went and began to prepare herself for the heavy work.[38] And I sent for the Hungarian wife of the controller of the royal household, Margit, who came immediately.[39] And there was another lady, named Frodnach, and I left both of them with my gracious lady and went directly to the mid-wife sent to us by the Lady of Schaunberg. She was asleep in the room of the little princess. I said to her: "Margret, get up right away, her grace is going to have the child." The woman answered me heavy with sleep and said: "Holy Cross, if we have a child today, there will be little chance that we go to Pressburg tomorrow." She did not want to get up, and since this struggle was taking too long, I rushed back to my noble lady to make sure that nothing was wrong with her, for the two women who were with her knew nothing about such matters. Then my gracious lady said: "Where is Margret?" And I told her grace the foolish answer the woman had given me. Then her grace said: "Hurry back to her and tell her to come. This is no joke." So I went back to the woman and chased her out of bed with angry words. And when she reached my noble lady, it did not even take half an hour before God the Almighty had a young king ready for us. Within the same hour in which the Holy Crown arrived from Plintenburg in Komorn, within that same hour King László was born.[40]

The mid-wife was shrewd. She said: "Noble lady, if you grant me whatever I ask for, I will tell you what I have here in my hands." The noble queen answered: "Yes, dear mother." And then the mid-wife said: "Gracious lady, I have a young king in my hands." Then the noble queen was happy and raised her hands to God and thanked God for His mercy.

When the new mother had been put into bed and everyone had left except only me, I kneeled down and spoke to the noble queen and said: "Gracious lady, your grace must thank God as long as you live for the great mercy and the miracle which God Almighty has bestowed on us by

---

[38] Hence, the delivery took place on a birthing stool as was usual at the time. According to contemporary medical treatises, medieval mid-wives held that a woman about to give birth should not sit on the stool until after the mouth of the uterus was touched and found to be open. Helene Kottanner probably knew this too. Cf. Helen Lemay, "Women and the Literature of Obstetrics and Gynecology," in *Medieval Women and the Sources of Medieval History*, ed. Joel T. Rosenthal (Athens: Univ. of Georgia Press, 1990), 189–210.

[39] I.e. the wife of Ladislaus Pelóczi. See 21, n. 7.

[40] Hence, Ladislaus Posthumous was born in the late night hours of 21 February 1440.

bringing the king and the Holy Crown together within the same hour."[41] Then the noble queen said: "Indeed, it is a great miracle from God Almighty, for it should not have happened earlier."

And when the ladies from Ofen learned that my lady had been delivered of the child, they were happy, as they ought to have been, but they were also annoyed that they had not been present at the birth and they strongly suspected that this was my doing, even though it truly was not my fault, for there simply had not been enough time. The king did not want to wait any longer; he wanted to rush to the Holy Crown before anyone else did, as if he had been told that the King of Poland was after his paternal heritage. And if he had slept one more week in his mother's body, he would have come to Pressburg, and they might not have been able to depart from there so soon or in peace, and then the Polish king might have reached Stuhlweissenburg before his grace did.[42] But if it is true that the Holy Crown was sent to the Holy Saint Stephen by God and meant by God for him, it is also true that it was clearly God's will that the true heir, King Lászlá, and not the King of Poland, should receive the Holy Crown of Hungary. There are certain people who ought to remember that.[43]

When the noble and loyal Count Ulrich Cillei learned that a king and friend had been born who was his nephew and lord, he and the lords from Croatia and the other magnates and the entire court were all overjoyed. The noble Count Cillei then ordered a bonfire, and they went on the river with torches and celebrated their joy until after midnight. Early the next morning, a message was sent to the Bishop of Gran, summoning him to come and assist with the baptism of the young king. He came, and the chaplain of Ofen named Master Franz came too. And my gracious lady expressed the wish that I be the child's godmother. But I said: "Gracious lady, I obey you in everything else, but I beg your grace, take Lady Margit."[44] And her grace did that.

As we were getting ready to baptize the noble king, we removed the black gown which Princess Elizabeth had been wearing to mourn the death of the noble and most precious King Albert and dressed her in a gown golden with red woven into it, and all the queen's ladies-in-waiting were also told to dress elegantly in honor of God, Who had given the country and the people a rightful king and lord. Then the most honorable

---

41 Notice the contrast here between the greediness of the mid-wife and Helene Kottanner's disinterested piety.

42 The coronation city. See 21, n. 1.

43 A direct reference to the opponents of Ladislaus Posthumous. See my discussion in the essay, 59.

44 A noblewoman. See 34, n. 39.

prelate, Lord Dionysus, Archbishop of Gran, took the young king and administered to him the sacrament of baptism and lifted him out of the font, and Count Bartholomeus of Croatia, and the Chaplain of Ofen, and Lady Margit, they all lifted the noble king out of the font. And they named him King Lászlá, which provoked the anger of some who were of the opinion that they should have called him King Peter, because that was the name he had brought with him.[45] Others thought that they should have named him King Albert in accordance with the will of his father, who was truly a pious king. But my gracious lady had made a vow to God and to the Holy King Saint Ladislaus, and she had sent offerings to Grosswardein, and she had also sent Vinsterel to the Holy Blood at Wilsnack with a larger silver statue of a child, and she had begged God to give her a son, so that she was bound by her promise and by the will of God.[46]

3.   When all this had happened, they sent out messengers to many places to announce that God Almighty had given the country and the people a king and heir, and the majority of the people rejoiced. Then the noble queen sent a special messenger to the Hungarian magnates who had been sent to the Polish king to tell them to return because God had given them an heir who would be king and no one else. But they refused to return and answered that they wanted to complete their mission and accomplish what they had been sent out to do, and so they continued on their way to the King of Poland. When the noble queen learned this, she was very distressed. Yet her faith in God remained strong, and she said that she knew well that God had not given her a son without a reason. The noble mother had no peace, for her affairs were of great weight and the magnates remained unwilling to make any concessions to her grace.

And many noblemen arrived. The Bishop of Raab came and offered his services to his natural lord.[47] The old Stephen Rozgónyi came too and also pledged his devotion to his natural lord.[48] And the Great Count, Lord Lawrence of Heidenreichsturn, came together with his wife.[49] And his wife gave the mid-wife four gold pieces, and they spoke many flattering

---

[45] The date of Ladislaus's baptism, 22 February, is Saint Peter's Day.

[46] In Grosswardein (Hung. Nagyvárad) both Saint Ladislaus (1077–1095) and Elizabeth's father, King Sigmund, lay buried. The cult of the Holy Blood in Wilsnack in Mark Brandenburg made it a very popular pilgrimage place between 1383 and 1532, drawing also numerous pilgrims from Hungary.

[47] Raab (Hung. Gyor) is about halfway between Pressburg and Stuhlweissenburg, approx. 35 km. from Komorn.

[48] A faithful follower and helper of Ladislaus's father, King Albert.

[49] Lawrence of Heidenreichsturn was Lord Palatine of Hungary from 1437 to 1447 – and at the same time leader of the Polish faction.

words. And the Great Count walked up to me as I stood beside the cradle and said: "Mother Kottanner, watch over him carefully; you have here a King of Hungary and a King of Bohemia, a Duke of Austria and a Margrave of Moravia, all in one." I answered him, saying: "My lord, I will watch over him as well as I can." And he spoke good and kind words to my gracious lady. But he was two-faced, as it turned out later on. Then the Great Count and his wife rode back to Ofen.

And the noble queen was beset by many worries, because there came numerous warnings that the young king's life was in danger, and we could not trust anyone. And I had to serve my gracious lady and also her children in anguish and with a heavy heart, and never during the entire time that her grace was bed-ridden, recovering from labor, did I undress, neither during the day nor during the night.

But when the time had come for the noble queen to proceed according to the customs of women, she took her son in her arms and carried him into the chapel at Komorn.[50] This took place four days after Easter [27 March 1440]. And the noble and loyal count Ulrich Cillei was constantly on my gracious lady's side and assisted her faithfully, and a duke of Lindbach, named Thomas Szécsi, also helped her faithfully until her death, as well as the Croatian counts, Count Bartholomeus and his brother, who were also loyal and came to her aid, and other counts and prelates and nobles; for there were nevertheless many noblemen as well as common people, both from the towns and the country, who were wholly devoted and loyal to her grace.

When the noble queen's confinement had come to an end and she was up again, the Hungarian magnates returned from their mission to the Polish king. Then Imre Marcali and Lord Matkó came to Komorn and Ladislaus Garai and several bishops as well as several counts and knights, and there also came a Bohemian lord named Smikosski. When the latter came to pay his respects to my gracious lady, he saw the young King Lászlá and without being asked he went to him and kneeled down in front of the cradle and holding up the two fingers of his right hand he swore fealty to the noble King Lászlá and his mother.

All that happened indeed, and when the noble queen heard that the lords Marcali and Matkó had returned from the Polish king, her grace

---

[50] ". . . according to the customs of women." Helene Kottanner may be referring here to an Austrian or Hungarian version of the "women's feast," a post-partum celebration of women well documented for other parts of Europe. On the practice in Scandinavia, see Grethe Jacobsen, "Pregnancy and Childbirth in the Medieval North," *Scandinavian Journal of History*, 9:2 (1984): 91–111; on the practice in France, see Natalie Zemon Davis, "Women on Top," in *Society and Culture in Early Modern Europe* (Palo Alto: Stanford Univ. Press, 1975), 124–151.

dressed carefully, choosing clothes which were festive yet appropriate for a widow. She did that because she wanted them to think that she was willing to marry the King of Poland, whom she really did not want, because she wanted to find out from them how they were planning to treat their natural sovereign. When these lords had assembled and wanted to have a meeting with her, my gracious lady refused to allow them into her residence and instead went outside to join them there, and so they had a conversation in front of the castle. And when the meeting was finished, her grace went back inside. But then she was warned that she should never go in front of the castle again if she did not want anything violent to happen to her. She followed this advice and allowed the lords to come into the castle while leaving their soldiers out front. So the negotiations took place inside the castle. And when all parties had put forth their position and my gracious lady also wanted to know their stand vis-a-vis their natural sovereign, King Lászlá, one of the two lords, either Matkó or Imre Marcali, spoke as follows: "Gracious lady, even if you had a son of ten years old, we would not accept him as our lord, because he could not lead us against the Turks." They remained of the opinion that she should marry the King of Poland. This saddened the noble queen deeply, but she did not show her true feelings to anyone and sought the advice of her friend, Count Ulrich Cillei, and of other loyal advisors to see what their position was in this matter. Then they recommended that she arrest the two lords, Matkó and Marcali.

And the noble queen handled this question very discreetly and wisely. And Lord Ladislaus Garai, her cousin, left without knowing anything about it.[51] And the two other lords wanted to get away as well and went to the other side of the Danube, to a little village straight across from Komorn, so that from the castle one could see them come and go.[52] Then my gracious lady announced that she planned to take up position in front of Totis and ordered Cillei's soldiers and those of Smikosski and of other vassals to sail across the Danube late at night.[53] My gracious lady rose early the next morning, at daybreak, and I took a torch, and together we went to a room on the battlements to see how the lords were faring. When it became light, we saw that these lords were assembling in a house. And then someone arrived from Ofen with four horses and that was John Ország of Guth, and he too went into the house and joined the lords. We saw all this from the wall. And not long thereafter, many soldiers approached on horseback. They were my gracious lady's soldiers, and they

---

51 Ladislaus Garai also sided with the Polish king.
52 This little village must have been Szöny.
53 Totis (Hung. Tata) is approx. 15 km. south of Komorn, in the same direction as Szöny.

surrounded the house and captured Lord Matkó and Lord Imre Marcali and their men, and the poor peasants fled from the village, barefoot and in their night shifts. And John Ország was captured too, and then these lords and their men were led into the ships which lay ready and then taken across the water to the queen's castle in Komorn, where they were imprisoned.

Then they demanded that Count Ulrich Cillei come to them; they wanted to give my gracious lady some good advice. And when Count Cillei went to see them, they urged my gracious lady to crown King Lászlá with the Holy Crown so that he would not be ousted from his realm. But they did not know that she had the Crown in her possession, for they knew no better than that it was at the Plintenburg stronghold with Lord Ladislaus Garai, who was on their side. And they hoped to regain their freedom in this manner.

When the noble Count Cillei brought the lords' message to my lady, she was pleased with their advice, and wanting to put her cousin, Lord Ladislaus, the Ban, to the test, she sent Lord Matthias, her Chancellor at that time, to Lord Ladislaus, the Ban, with the message that he should give her the Crown because she wanted to have her son crowned and grant him possession of his paternal heritage.[54] Lord Ladislaus answered that he would gladly do that, but only on the condition that she would release Lord Matkó and Lord Imre Marcali. My gracious lady was pleased with this answer, but now she worried that her cousin, Lord Ladislaus, the Ban, would be unfavorably disposed toward her if he found out that she already had the Holy Crown, and she secretly took me aside and spoke to me as follows: "Dear mother Kottanner, what would you advise me to do? Lord Ladislaus has said that he is willing to give me the Crown; how could I return it to Plintenburg again?"

When I heard this, I was so shaken by my wise lady's change of heart that I felt it in all my limbs, and I thought by myself that this must be an idea inspired by the Devil. I could hardly control myself and answered angrily and spoke as follows: "Woman, stop that! I will not do it and will not risk my life like that and will not even help you with advice, for it is always better to be in the bushes than in the stocks.[55] You can always return it later, but whoever is your friend now may well become your enemy later." When the noble queen heard me answer her so rudely, out of anger, she kept silent and said neither yes nor no and left me thus, without receiving an answer to her question, and also later she never talked to me about it again. Had the Crown remained at Plintenburg this

54 Lord Matthias Gathalóczi, Bishop of Wesprim.
55 A proverb roughly equivalent to: "Better freezing outside than warm in jail"?

long, it surely would have fallen into the hands of the Polish king, as you will hear hereafter. Notice, though, how diligent the Devil was in the very beginning and towards the end.

Not long thereafter, the Lord of Freistadt, Voivode Nicholas Ujláki, came to my gracious lady and said he wanted to serve her grace, and her grace made him Captain of Stuhlweissenburg.[56] Shortly after that we received the news, which turned out to be accurate, that the King of Poland was on his way and planning to go to Ofen, as indeed happened, and so we quickly and secretly made preparations for the coronation.

My gracious lady sent for a golden cloth to be brought from Ofen which would be used for King Lászlá's coronation gown, but the messenger took too much time and we worried that it would take too long because the coronation had to take place on a church holiday. That would be on Pentecost, the first upcoming holiday [15 May 1440], which was not far off, so we had to hurry. But there happened to be a beautiful and large vestment which had belonged to Emperor Sigmund; it was red and golden with silver-white spots worked into it. We cut it up and made out of it the young king's very first ceremonial dress, which he would wear together with the Holy Crown. And now tell me if this would not be a sign that he was meant to rule over the inheritance of both his father and his mother, for their coats of arms both have red and white in them.[57] I sewed the little gown, the alb, the humeral veil and the stole, the maniples, the gloves, and the shoes, and I had to make them secretly, in the chapel, behind locked doors.

When everything was ready, my gracious lady sent Lord Matthias, her Chancellor, to her cousin, Lord Ladislaus, the Ban, with the message that he should join her and accompany her to Stuhlweissenburg, because she was going to have her son crowned and that she had the Holy Crown in her possession. When Lord Ladislaus, the Ban, heard this, he was not pleased at all, but he kept hoping that it was not true, that the Crown was still at Plintenburg, and he did not join my gracious lady. When her grace learned that Lord Ladislaus was not coming, her grace sent the two lords, Matkó and Imre Marcali, to Ödenburg. And she sent with them a knight, a vassal of Cillei's named Henry of Randegg, to watch them, because Count Ulrich Cillei was at the time in charge of Ödenburg and he had placed a warden in the town, whose name was Frederick Flednitzer, and to this man's supervision she entrusted these lords.[58]

---

56 Wojwode, like Banus, designates a function in Hungarian local administration.
57 Red and white were the colors of Albert and Elizabeth's families. They occur together several times in the course of the story, which Helene Kottanner interprets as symbolic of divine support for the Habsburgs.
58 Actually, Christopher Flednitzer.

Then the noble queen sent a messenger in utmost secrecy to the noble sovereign of Austria named Duke Albert and announced to him that she intended to have my gracious lord, King Lászlá, crowned on the day of Pentecost [15 May 1440].[59] The noble sovereign, Duke Albert, proved to be the truly loyal friend one can count on in extremity, and he quickly mounted his horse and rode to Stuhlweissenburg in such haste that his men rode several horses to death, and on Pentecost he presented himself in person to his nephew, King Lászlá. And had it been necessary, he would have sacrificed his own life for his sake.

When all the servants and lords who were to accompany my gracious lady to Stuhlweissenburg had assembled, her grace sent a message to the Archbishop of Gran, requesting him to come and ride with her to Stuhlweissenburg to attend her son's coronation. He came with a large following. And when the cradle in which the young king would be carried was ready, we needed always four men to carry his grace. And on the Thursday afternoon [12 May 1440] before Pentecost, the noble queen rode off with the young king and the noble Count Cillei and the Croatian counts and the dukes of Lindbach. And the Great Count, Lord Lawrence of Heidenreichsturn, also joined my gracious lady's train.

A large vessel of the kind called flatbottom lay prepared. The noble queen and her royal offspring, both son and daughter, as well as a great many people of quality got in, so that the vessel became very full and was so heavy that it was hardly one hand above the water, which was dangerous and risky. But then there came a strong wind, and God helped us joyously across the water.

And when we reached the other side, they carried the young king in the cradle – for there were always four armed men to carry him – and I, his servant, rode beside the cradle. But when they had carried him only a little while, he began to cry loudly and would not stay in the cradle. So I stepped down from my horse and carried him in my arms. It rained so hard that I had trouble walking, but there was a pious knight, named Hanns of Pielach, who guided me through the puddles. It was already very dark when we reached Totis, and we stayed there for the night. The next morning, I rode in front with the young king, while my gracious lady stayed in the back with her youngest daughter, because her grace had business to discuss with the Great Count, who spoke flattering words to her and said that he had led his army honorably and was willing to bring it to its death honorably as well. This was all a sham, however, for he really did not want to travel with her grace to Stuhlweissenburg and turned

---

[59] Albert VI, Duke of Austria (1418–1463), second cousin of Elizabeth's husband, and brother of Archduke Frederick V.

around mid-way and rode off to Ofen to await the arrival of the Polish king.

And as I rode in front with the young king, we arrived at a beautiful hunting lodge, the German name of which is Grintsechdel.[60] Since we were going to stay there for the night, we would have liked to eat, but we did not find much, because it was Friday and we were supposed to fast. And we stayed there for the night and waited for my gracious lady to catch up with us.

Then we traveled on to Stuhlweissenburg. When we were almost there, the Lord of Freistadt, Nicholas Ujláki, rode out to meet us with at least five hundred horses.[61] When we went through the marshland, the young king began to cry and wanted to stay neither in the cradle nor in the carriage. And I had to carry his grace in my arms until we were inside the city of Stuhlweissenburg. Then the lords dismounted from their horses and formed a wide circle of armored men, holding naked swords in their hands, and into the middle of that circle I, Helene Kottanner, had to carry the young king, with on one side Count Bartholomeus of Croatia and on the other side someone else, and both accompanied me in honor of the noble king, and so we went through the city until we were inside the inn. That was on the eve of Pentecost [14 May 1440].

Then my gracious lady summoned the oldest citizens, who have to be present, and showed them the Holy Crown and ordered them to proceed according to the tradition and as had always been done. And there were some among these citizens who remembered that Emperor Sigmund had been crowned there too and who had been present at his coronation.[62]

On the morning of the day of Pentecost [15 May 1440], I rose early and bathed the noble king and prepared him as well as I could. Then they carried him into the church where all kings are crowned. And many persons of quality, ecclesiastics as well as lay people, were present there, as you have heard before. And when we had entered the church, they carried the young king to the choir. But the door to the choir was closed, and the citizens were inside, while my gracious lady stood outside the door with her son, the noble king. And then my gracious lady spoke to them in Hungarian, and the citizens likewise answered her grace back in Hungarian. They said that her grace should swear the oath on behalf of her son, the noble king, for on that day his grace was exactly twelve weeks

60 Hung. Gerencsér. Kottanner's story indicates that there lived in 1440 in this area of the Schilberg mountains Germans from whom she learned these German place names. Cf. Mollay, 59 n. 120.
61 Wojwode Nicholas Ujláki, whom Elizabeth had made Captain of Stuhlweissenburg shortly before. See 40.
62 Sigmund was crowned in Stuhlweissenburg on 31 March 1387.

old.[63] When this had been done according to their old custom, they opened the door and admitted their natural lord and lady as well as the other people, clergy and laymen, who had been summoned to attend. And the young queen, the Lady Elizabeth, stood upstairs, near the organ, so that she would not get hurt in the crowd, for she was not yet four years old.

When they were about to celebrate the Mass, I had to lift up the young king and hold his grace while they confirmed him. And Nicholas Ujláki, the Lord of Freistadt, had been appointed to dub the young king a knight and thus make him rightly a true lord of the realm. And the noble Count Cillei had a sword all mounted with silver and gold, on which was written the motto: "Invincible." And this same sword he presented to the young king so that with it he could be made a knight. Then I, Helene Kottanner, took the king in my arms, and the Lord of Freistadt took the sword in his hand and made the king a knight, but he hit him so hard with the sword that I could feel the blow in my arm. The noble queen, who stood beside me, had noticed this, and she said to the Lord of Freistadt: "Az istenért, még ne sértsd!" which means: "For God's sake, don't hurt him."[64] Then he said: "Nem," which means: "No," and he laughed. Then the Right Reverend Prelate, Archbishop of Gran, took the holy oil and anointed the noble royal child king. Then they dressed him in the golden gown that is worn by all kings. Then the archbishop took the Holy Crown and placed it on the head of the noblest king who ever lived in holy Christendom, King Lászlá, son of King Albert, grandson of Emperor Sigmund, who was crowned with the Holy Crown in Stuhlweissenburg on the holy day of Pentecost by the Archbishop of Gran.

For they have three laws in the kingdom of Hungary, and if a monarch fails to observe even one of them, the people refuse to acknowledge him as their rightful king. The first law requires that the king of Hungary be crowned with the Holy Crown. The second, that he be crowned by the Archbishop of Gran. The third, that the coronation take place in Stuhlweissenburg.[65] All three laws were carefully observed in the case of the noble King Ladislaus, and on the day on which his grace was crowned, he was exactly twelve weeks old. And you probably know that as the Archbishop placed the Holy Crown on the child's head and held it there,

---

[63] The oath probably concerned the rights and privileges of the citizens of Stuhlweissenburg which Elizabeth had to guarantee. Cf. Mollay, 60 n. 122.

[64] Actually, Kottanner's phonetic rendition is: "Istemere nem misserten."

[65] The "laws" enumerated and described here were in reality unwritten rules, legal traditions which, with the exception of the first one, were observed without interruption from 1001 to 1526. The only Hungarian king who was not crowned with the Holy Crown of Saint Stephen was Elizabeth's opponent Wladislaus, King of Poland, who was crowned by the Archbishop of Gran on 17 July 1440, only two months after the Archbishop had crowned Elizabeth's son.

he held up his head with the strength of a one-year-old, and that is rarely seen in children of twelve weeks.

When the noble King Lászlá had been crowned in my arms at the altar of Saint Stephen, I carried the noble king up a small flight of stairs to a platform, as is the tradition there. Then they read the coronation charter, which is part of the ceremony. For this they needed a golden cloth for the king to sit on, as is the custom there. Therefore, to comply with this rule, I took from his cradle a cover, red and golden and banded with white ermine. And notice how the colors red and white once again came together by chance.[66] Then the noble king was held on the golden cloth and Count Ulrich Cillei held the Crown over his head until we finished singing the Mass. But the noble young king had little joy of his coronation, for he cried so loud that it could be heard throughout the entire church and the common people marveled and said that it was not the voice of a child of twelve weeks but rather of a one-year-old, which he really was not. Then the lord of Freistadt, Nicholas Ujláki, bestowed knighthood on behalf of the noble King Lászlá.

When the Mass was over, I carried the noble king down again and laid him in the cradle because he was tired after being held up for so long. Then they carried him into St. Peter's Church, where I had to lift him out of the cradle once more and carry him to a chair and put him down on it, as is the custom there; for every king who is crowned there must sit on that chair.[67] Then I carried his grace down again and put him back in the cradle. Then they carried the noble king out of St. Peter's Church, and the royal family followed on foot behind him until we reached the inn. Only the noble Count Ulrich Cillei rode his horse, because he had to carry the Holy Crown and hold it over the noble king's head so that all could see that it was the Holy Crown which had been worn by the Holy King, Saint Stephen, and the other kings of Hungary.

And Count Bartholomeus carried the apple, and the Duke of Lindbach, named Thomas Szécsi, carried the scepter. Another nobleman walked in front of the king with the legate staff, to show that no part of Hungary is a fief of the Holy Roman Empire.[68] They also held by his side the sword with which his grace had been knighted. And they threw coins among the crowd. And the noble queen felt such awe for her son and was so meek, that I, humble woman, had priority over her grace that day and was to remain closest to the noble king, because I had held his grace in my arms during his holy anointment and coronation.

[66] See 40, n. 57.

[67] Actually the name of the church was St. Peter and St. Paul.

[68] This is untrue. In reality, the coronation insignia had remained in the Plintenburg treasure vault and could not have been displayed here. See essay, 55–56.

And the illustrious sovereign of Austria, Duke Albert, had hurried to Stuhlweissenburg to serve and to assist the most illustrious sovereign, King Lászlá, his nephew. Thus the noble sovereign, Duke Albert, proved the natural law that blood relations do not abandon each other in extremity.

When the noble king had returned to the inn and found some quiet there, he was exhausted from having been carried around so long. When the lords and everyone else had gone away, the noble queen was left alone with her son. Then I kneeled down in front of the noble queen and reminded her grace of the services I had rendered her grace as well as to the noble king and to her grace's other children, to the entire royal family. Then the noble queen offered me her hand and said: "Stand up. If it happens that God grants that everything goes well and our difficulties are resolved, I will elevate you and all your family. You have truly deserved that, for you have done for me and my children more than I would have been capable or in the position to do myself." Then I bowed down with great humility and thanked her grace for this great comfort.

When all this had happened, we received the news that the Polish king was in the vicinity of Ofen and about to cross the Danube in order to make his entrance into the main city, as indeed happened. But when the Pole arrived at the walls of Ofen, the townspeople refused to let him in. Then the Great Count let him in through the castle.[69] And that is when the two faces of the Great Count, Lord Lawrence of Heidenreichsturn, who had been double-dealing for a long time, became clearly visible. When the noble queen learned this, she consulted with her friends and the noble lords who were with her at that time. They recommended that she send her soldiers to Ofen and have them besiege the main city, for they would find the Pole and his men unprepared for an attack, which was in fact the case.

Then Count Ulrich Cillei and other members of the royal party gathered their troops and set out thither. But then someone among the people said: "While those in front attack the Polish king, we will meanwhile attack those in the back." This came to the ears of Cillei, who then refused to go any further and turned around mid-way and went back to Stuhlweissenburg. Whether those words were meant as a warning or rather as a ruse, God surely knows, for He knows our hearts, but if they had continued on their way, they would indeed have found the Pole unaware of any danger.

When the Polish king learned that they had planned to attack him, he

---

[69] Wladislaus, the Polish king, entered Ofen on 21 May and stayed until 15 July. During this time Ladislaus Garai gave him the Plintenburg stronghold. Cf. Mollay, 61 n. 131.

spoke the following words: "But I did not come out here because I wanted to fight, I came out here because I wanted to dance and make merry, for if I didn't, Duke Albert would."[70] He said this because the noble sovereign, Duke Albert, was there to assist my noble lady and the noble King Ladislaus, his nephew. However, he had not come because he wanted to dance, he had come in case it were necessary for him to wield his sword and risk his life for the sake of his friend, and he certainly would have done that had something happened to King Lászlá.

4.   Then they decided to take the noble king to some place near Stuhl-weissenburg, but on account of the enemy's presence they did not know where. There happened to be two bishops among the queen's company; one was the Bishop of Raab, the other the Bishop of Wesprim. The lords then advised to take the noble King Lászlá to Wesprim, because it was closer by. They sent a message to Wesprim, but then the vassals in charge of Wesprim would accept neither the king nor the queen. And they suspected that the bishop was partly responsible for that. But it was all God's will, indeed, for if they had agreed to take us in, we surely would have left to go there and then the enemy would have encircled us like David in the town of Ceila.[71]

Then the lords suggested that they take the noble king to Raab and they spoke with the Bishop of Raab.[72] The bishop stated his willingness to take in his natural liege and lady. And he said that even if the Devil sat on God's right-hand side, he would have to acknowledge that King Lászlá is the rightful heir and king of Hungary. Then we readied ourselves for the journey through the country to Raab.

When it was evening and everybody had gone to bed, my gracious lady sent to me the noble Lady Margit with the message that I should go to her grace immediately. This frightened me and it made me think that there must be some contretemps. The noble queen was alone, walking back and forth absorbed in thought, and she said to me: "Well, what would you advise me now? We are having problems. They want to dictate a hiding place for the Holy Crown, but if it falls in the hands of the enemy, nothing good will come of it." We talked about the matter for a long time. And since we were staying at the Brobsthof and there was a little walled-in garden there, I said: "Gracious lady, let us bury it in the garden and even

---

70 Albert VI of Austria (cf. 41, n. 59) was well known for his love of pleasure and his excessive lifestyle. Wladislaus is suggesting that the duke came for the festivities, not out of loyalty or love for the king.

71 Ceila, nowadays Kîla, is a village on the way to Hebron. David had to flee from there to escape encirclement by Saul. Kings 1:23, 27–31.

72 See 36, n. 47.

if this place should be lost to the enemy, we will always be able to find a way to get into the garden over the wall."[73] But then the wise queen said: "I have thought about that too, but I do not find it a good idea because someone might think that the Holy Crown were lost." Then I withdrew for a short while to think this over and I appealed to the Mother of Mercy to obtain for us her Son's mercy so that we would handle this matter wisely and no evil would come of it. Then I returned to the noble queen and said: "Gracious lady, unsurpassed indeed is your wisdom. The following solution seems best to me: Her grace knows well that the king is worth more than the Holy Crown. Therefore, let us put the Holy Crown in the cradle underneath the king, and wherever God sends the king, the Crown will go too." Her grace liked this advice and said: "This is what we shall do, and we shall let you take care of it."

The next morning, I took the Holy Crown, wrapped it carefully in a cloth and then placed it in the cradle underneath the straw – because his grace did not sleep on feathers yet – and next to it I put a long spoon of the kind that is used to make mash for babies. I did that so that if anyone were to reach into the cradle, they would think that what lay there was something to prepare the noble king's food with, and no one knew anything about this at that time except my noble lady and myself.

And when we were ready for our journey through the country to Raab, we had a large number of mounted knights and also many foot soldiers and went on our way. And we had many troubles, because the peasants had deserted their villages and fled to the forest of the Schildberg mountains and most of them belonged to lords who were hostile to us.[74] When we began to approach the Schildberg mountains, I stepped down from my horse and took the noble king out of the cradle and put him in the carriage in which the noble queen sat with her young daughter, Princess Elizabeth. And we, maids-of-honor and ladies-in-waiting, formed a circle around the royal family, so that if anyone were to shoot at the carriage, we could hold off the shots. And we had a large number of foot soldiers walking on both sides of the carriage, who were searching the bushes for enemy soldiers hiding in the woods who might want to harm us. And with the help of God we thus crossed the Schildberg mountains unharmed.

Then I took the noble king out of the carriage again and put him back into the cradle, and I rode beside the cradle. They had not carried him

---

[73] Another inn.

[74] Actually, in 1440 this area was in the hands of Stephen Rozgónyi, a supporter of the queen. If the peasants fled to the mountains at the approach of Queen Elizabeth's large train, almost 2000 people on foot and horseback, it was for fear of the Bohemian and German soldiers whose violence and brutality were well known.

very far, however, when he began to cry loudly and would not stay in his cradle nor in the carriage, nor could the wet-nurse get him to calm down. Then I took him in my arms and carried him a good part of the way and the wet-nurse walked with me, until both of us grew tired. Then I laid him in his cradle again.

And all the while we were traveling through the country, the weather kept changing. At times it rained so hard that the noble king got thoroughly wet, for we were not equipped for a long journey but only for a short one. But I had brought along a fur coat in case we should need it in an emergency, and when it rained heavily, I put it over the cradle until it was completely wet and then I had it rubbed dry and then spread it out over the cradle again, and I did this as long as it kept raining. At other times, the wind was so strong that it beat into the cradle and the noble king could hardly open his eyes. Then, sometimes, it was again so hot, that he perspired all over and was covered with drops of sweat, and then he got little blisters on his skin from the heat. All this the noble king had to endure while we were traveling through the country.

And when we had reached the inn and it was almost night and all had eaten, the knights lay down all around the house in which the royal family was to spend the night and made a fire and kept watch during the night, as is the custom in the kingdom of Hungary.

The next day we traveled on to Raab. And when we had almost reached Raab, it was already completely dark. And then we had to wait before Raab until it was almost midnight. And the noble sovereign of Austria, Duke Albert, kept on one side of the cradle, close to the noble king, his nephew, and I rode on the other. Suddenly, there was a well in front of me which I had not seen because it was so dark. Then the humility and great nobility of the noble sovereign came out with full force, and he warned me and said: "Woman, there is a well in front of you, beware that you don't fall into it with your horse."

And during the entire time that we stopped there the noble Count Ulrich Cillei was with the noble queen and they talked together about our accommodations in the city; who should stay in the castle, and who inside the town, or in front of the town. And there was some disagreement between the Hungarians and the Germans, for both groups would have liked to be inside the town. But finally the bishop allowed the royal family and several counts and lords into the castle. And for me they lowered a little bridge, and we had to hurry across it, and then they pulled it back up again immediately behind us. And the lords who had come in with us never took off their armor that night.

And we had not been in Raab for very long when several Bohemian nobles came to Raab who wanted to see their natural lord, and so I had to present the noble king to them, naked on a pillow. Then they all cheered and laughed so hard that the child got frightened and began to weep loudly. Now it so happened that there was a little circumcised boy there who was dressed like a court fool, although he was not one. And whenever the noble king would not be quiet, the boy would go to the cradle and sing and play on the luth, and then the noble king stopped crying instantly.

Meanwhile, many noblemen arrived in Raab. And every time my gracious lady needed to discuss something urgently in a secret meeting, her grace sent for Duke Albert and for Cillei, and this began to aggravate the Lord of Freistadt, Nicholas Ujláki, who became hostile because he was not included in the secret talks too. There was also an Hungarian lord in my lady's company at the time, whose name was Hederich of Heiden-reichsturn, who had a brother who was Abbot of St. Martinsberg monas-tery. And my gracious lady asked this Lord Hederich of Heidenreichsturn if he would help her against his brother, the abbot, by giving her control over St. Martinsberg for the duration of the war, for it was like a bastion before Ofen. Her grace was partly satisfied on this point and she sent Count Ulrich Cillei to the Abbot of St. Martinsberg with a message. But then some small incident happened which disturbed her plan. Where the Devil does not like to go himself he sends his messenger.

We stayed in Raab for almost three weeks and were troubled by many worries, and one night I dreamed that the Holy Crown had fallen into a dirt pit and was full of stains. As soon as I woke up the next morning, I went to the noble queen and told her my dream about the Holy Crown. This frightened her grace and she said: "That dream means something." And she immediately went to the place where the Holy Crown was and examined it carefully, but she did not see anything wrong with it.

5.   Then the lords decided that it was unwise for the noble royal family to stay together, that they should be separated, and several of them advised to take King Lászlá to Ödenburg, while others advised to take him to Forchtenstein, and they advised that they leave my young mistress in Raab.[75] My husband, Kottanner, was assigned to her grace's service, and he too had to swear loyalty on the reliquary, as is the custom in Hungary. The lords further suggested that my gracious lady go and stay in Press-burg. Then the noble queen said to me: "What do you advise, dear mother Kottanner? If I could divide you in three parts, I would gladly do it. I would like to keep you to myself, and I would also like to leave you with my son, and I would also like to see you staying with my daughter." Then she consulted with the lords to see which party I should accompany. Then

[75] Forchtenstein is even further west than Ödenburg.

the lords wanted nothing else but that I should stay with the noble king. This did not make me happy, for I understood that my service would be even more difficult and my worries greater than before, because I would not be in the presence of my gracious lady.

Now some lords were talking about sending the noble king to Trentschin, where he would be sufficiently safe, for the two castles of Trentschin and Pluntsch were at that time both in the hands of the Lord of Ellerbach. But because of the enemy's presence there, they could not take the noble king there.[76] Then the noble queen sent for me and said: "Dear mother Kottanner, what do you advise me; where should I take my son?" Then I advised her grace as it was my duty and I said: "Gracious lady, take him wherever you want, but for his sake take him only to a place that is in your hands and beware of the kings." Then the noble queen said: "You are right," and went and discussed with the lords where she should take her son, the noble king. Then the lords advised her to send him to Ödenburg which also belonged to the Holy Crown of Hungary and had a key position in the country and over which my gracious lady and Count Ulrich Cillei had complete control at that time. And they left it at this.

Then they composed the king's retinue and summoned those who were to accompany him. One of them was Lord Franz of Pöker, a pious and reliable man. Another was a pious knight named Lord Pancras of Tengold. The third was also a pious nobleman, a Croate named Thomas Gerzúksi. And there were also two chamberlains, one called Sigmund Abdacher, the other Heinrich Knocht. And they had twenty-four horses all in all. And I, Helene Kottanner, and the wet-nurse, too, went and prayed before the statue of the Virgin. I was reluctant to go on that journey and went to tell my gracious lady about the anguish I felt. Then my grace spoke many kind words to me and comforted me well and said: "By all means go, and let the most precious treasure I have under the sun be entrusted to your care. And even if I have only one penny left, I will share it with you."

And when we were ready to leave, her grace sent a messenger to Count Ulrich Cillei and to the Bishop of Raab and summoned all the knights and soldiers who had been assigned to the service of the king, and she took one after the other into the room, separately, and they all had to swear loyalty, even the wet-nurse and the other women I had with me. They all had to swear on the reliquary, as is the custom in Hungary, except only me; I was the only one who didn't, because her grace had complete confidence in me. Then they sent us the noble and loyal Ulrich of Eitzing who was willing and prepared to lead us to Ödenburg.

---

76 Trentschin (Hung. Trencin) is way up north along the river Waag. Pluntsch (Hung. Beckó) is just south of Trentschin.

And when we were about to depart, the noble queen took leave of her son, the noble King Lászlá, and also of his sister, Princess Elizabeth, and she began to shake. And I too said good-bye with grief in my heart, because it was difficult for me to leave the noble queen and because I had raised the young princess conscientiously and with love. And along with the royal family I also had to leave behind my husband and my daughter Katharina.

And we set out on our journey with great anguish in our hearts, and it took a great deal of effort and hard work, for it had rained very hard and the puddles were deep, and we had to carry the noble king in his cradle through the mud and, the men who carried him were wading up to their knees through the water.

The noble king had left the Holy Crown behind in Raab, but there were many people who knew no better than that we were carrying the Holy Crown with us too.[77] And when we had gone barely three hours in the direction of Altenburg, the noble and loyal Lord Ulrich of Eitzing rode up to me and said: "What do you advise, dear mother Kottanner? My gracious lady has ordered us to stop for the night in the next village, but it belongs to the Great Count and, moreover, there is no one there, which is suspicious. If it is not too much for my lord, we would prefer to carry him further." Then I spoke: "I agree that we should not stay here; we will carry him as far as we can until we come to a place where we will be safe."

Then we went on to Altenburg. And before we had reached the inn, a messenger came to us from Raab, who told us the news that there had been a great assembly of people at Raab and that a soldier of my Lord Cillei's had been killed. And then some soldiers in our company, who would not let their hands get out of the habit, rode off the road to steal cattle from the poor peasants and brought it all into the courtyard of the inn where we were staying. But the lords appointed to my master's service found this very unwise, and they said to me: "It is not good that our Lord, King Lászlá, should be known as a robber in his young days without it being his or our fault." Then I sent a message to the noble and loyal Lord Ulrich of Eitzing and told him this and asked him if he would see to it that these poor people be given their cattle back, that this would greatly please my gracious lady, as I knew very well, for many of these poor people were supporters of the queen. Then the noble and loyal Lord Ulrich of Eitzing acted wisely, and he sent someone to the judge and ordered the market gate to be closed until the cattle had been returned to the poor

---

[77] Queen Elizabeth took the Holy Crown with her to Vienna where she pawned it to Frederick III.

people; for they were in front of the house, clamoring loudly, claiming their lifestock. And there were some who did not like it at all that they had to return the cattle, and these men came from the German provinces. And we stayed there for the night.

The next morning, we left and traveled to Neusiedl, which took us until after midnight. But the following morning we went on our way again and continued until we approached the little village.[78] There, the church bells were ringing to welcome the noble king, and the people came out in a procession, carrying the reliquary, and confirmed their loyalty to their natural master. And there were even two noble ladies who walked in front of the reliquary in the procession.

But when we were almost across from Eisenstadt, we became very concerned because we were told that a great train of travelers had come into Eisenstadt and that they were enemies. It was raining hard, and we kept silent and were full of fear. But when we approached Ödenburg, many people, men and women, came out of the city with the reliquary to come and meet the noble king and to welcome him as their natural lord. And when we had arrived in Ödenburg, we decided to stop there and rest.

And you should know that on the night of our arrival, there was such a flood that not a single person in the entire area could remember ever having seen such a great rush of water before. And, indeed, you must know too that the noble king cried a great deal that night and was so restless that I had a more difficult night with him than I had had in a long time.

And not long afterwards the news came that the king of Poland had captured Count Ulrich Cillei, and then we were very sad about the state of our affairs, for we knew well that this meant a great loss of land and people to my lord and lady. And not long thereafter, we received the grievous news that the honorable prelate, the bishop of Gran, and Lord Ladislaus Garai, the Ban, had been captured and made prisoners while they were with an escort on their way to the Polish king, who wanted them to help him get crowned king of the kingdom of Hungary, for they were wondering if the Holy Crown was not still at the Plintenburg stronghold, because the seals and the locks were still in place on the doors . . .

[78] This little village was probably Jois. Cf. Mollay, 63 n. 157.

Interpretative Essay

"And I, Helene Kottanner, . . ."
Kottanner's *Memoirs* as Autobiography

The scholarly process of searching for the historical self of women is fraught with difficulties. With respect to the late-medieval period, by far the greatest difficulty is that the textual record, mostly produced by men, has a strong masculinist bias. Very few women were literate, and if a woman did know how to read and write and actually felt the urge to express herself in writing, she often did so privately or even secretly. Only nuns, mystics, and noblewomen occasionally produced work meant for eyes other than their own. In the course of the years that have passed since, moreover, many manuscripts were destroyed or lost. As a result, the number of female-authored texts dating from this period available to us now is extremely small.

Yet some historians feel that "attempts to map the range and variety of women's subjective experiences cannot be based on the textual evidence left by the extraordinary few whose proximity to power and influence allowed them to write and publish."[1] They see the disproportionate representation of noble and wealthy women among the literate in the Middle Ages as a problem and therefore prefer a contextual critical approach to confront "the vexed relationship between the lives of 'real' women and the ideological representation of them in what remains of the textual tradition."[2] In other words, these historians favor the study of social context, of contemporary economic, legal, political and religious systems, as a way to assess the literary constructions of women in the male-authored tradition against the materiality of women's lives as it is reflected in these contextual materials.[3]

Perhaps this kind of distrust of texts written by, or about, elite women is one reason why Helene Kottanner's *Memoirs* have suffered scholarly neglect, even from those with a special interest in women's literature. The

1 Sheila Fisher and Janet E. Halley, eds., "The Lady Vanishes: The Problem of Women's Absence in Late Medieval and Renaissance Texts," in *Seeking the Woman in Late Medieval and Renaissance Writings: Essays in Contextual Criticism* (Knoxville: Univ. of Tennessee Press, 1989), 3.
2 Ibid., 1.
3 Ibid., 6–7.

"history from below" movement, at any rate, has led to increased attention, among medievalists as well, for popular culture and the social conditions of the lower classes, whereas for several decades themes involving political elites, regal authority, and coronation rituals were unpopular, if they were not considered altogether irrelevant. A renewed critical interest in the issues of power, hierarchy, and rulership as well as in medieval queens and noblewomen may explain Helene Kottanner's inclusion in some recent German studies of medieval women writers.[4] However, in these studies, the *Memoirs* are dealt with superficially and their literary and textual aspects virtually ignored.

While we cannot hope to retrieve fully "the range and variety of women's subjective experiences" in the late-medieval period, we must nevertheless continue to treasure what textual evidence is left of the few women who did write, even if these women belonged to a privileged elite and even if their authorship was made possible by their "proximity to power and influence." It is serious enough that women are mostly absent from the textual record; we cannot afford to ignore or neglect the possible referential and representative value of what presence they do have.

Of course, "the historical self of women is an. . . elusive subject of study." We should neither simplify women's presence in history, nor "create them in our own image, or romanticize their occlusion by 'restoring' them."[5] But when we are so lucky as to come upon a unique ego-document like Helene Kottanner's *Memoirs*, we must read it carefully and make an attempt to recreate at least one woman, the one whose voice reaches us across the centuries, in the image she gives, both consciously and unconsciously, of herself. Her "proximity to power and influence" should not disqualify her from having representative value in some respects, particularly when it comes to gender roles and relations, for the text of these *Memoirs* gives expression both to a historical self, the subjective self of the rather exceptional burgher woman Helene Kottanner, and to a value system whose parameters demarcate, if not necessarily the fields of activity or the sense of self of late-medieval

---

4   See János M. Bak, ed., intro. to *Coronations: Medieval and Early Modern Monarchic Ritual* (Berkeley: Univ. of California Press, 1990), 10; Ursula Liebertz-Grün, "Frau und Herrscherin. Zur Sozialisation deutscher Adeliger (1150–1450)," in *Auf der Suche nach der Frau im Mittelalter*, ed. Bea Lundt (Munich: Wilhelm Fink, 1991), 184–187; Ursula Liebertz-Grün, "Höfische Autorinnen von der karolingischen Kulturreform bis zum Humanismus," in *Deutsche Literatur von Frauen* Bd 1, ed. Gisela Brinker-Gabler (Munich: C. H. Beck, 1988), 39–64; about Helene Kottanner, 60–63; Ursula Liebertz-Grün, "Autorinnen im Umkreis der Höfe," in *Frauen Literatur Geschichte*, ed. Hiltrud Gnug and Renate Mohrmann (Stuttgart: J. B. Metzlersche Verlagsbuchhandlung, 1985), 16–34; about Kottanner, 33.

5   *Seeking the Woman*, 13.

Austrian-Hungarian women, certainly their modes of self-representation and the criteria according to which they were judged by their contemporaries.

While Kottanner's *Memoirs* do not constitute an autobiographical document properly speaking – lacking a conscious preoccupation with the I's unique, personal inner world of thought, feeling, and sensation – they constitute nonetheless a literary form of self-definition and self-revelation. For "the memorialist's vision of the outer world is as much a projection and refraction of the self as the autobiographer's. The manifest content of the memoir may be different, but the latent content is likewise self-revelation."[6]

As Freud and Lacan observed and as is illustrated by most autobiographical texts, the self only becomes a meaningful concept when viewed through the provision of an "Other" or others. While male autobiography may be seen as using a mostly implied, imagined "Other," namely Woman, to define and confirm the male subject, female autobiography more often than not emphasizes an explicit, genuinely experienced relation or relations of self to a significant other or others, often a man, a lover, husband, or father, but also frequently women, a mother, an aunt, or other female role models.[7] To decide whether this "delineation of identity through alterity" marks the "difference" of autogynography and is a reflection of the female I, which, as some feminist critics contend, is not a "totalized self-contained subject present to itself," as is the male self created by the phallocentric Western myth of subjecthood, but rather "composed of threads and life lines extending to others," would far exceed the limits of this essay.[8] For my purpose, it is sufficient to note that any discourse, explicit or implied, about others reflects and refracts aspects of the self. Hence, we can read the *Memoirs* of Helene Kottanner, whose explicit focus is on certain political events and on the narrator's relation with another woman, Queen Elizabeth, as a "projection and refraction" of the narrator's self, of the subjective self of a late-medieval woman, whose identity and referential status we must approach with caution yet cannot afford to ignore.

Because historians of the period have attributed a high degree of accuracy, in other words "truth value" or referentiality, to Kottanner's text when it comes to the events and rituals she describes, it is tempting

6 Marcus K. Bilson and Sidonie A. Smith, "Lilian Hellman and the Strategy of the Other," in *Women's Autobiography*, ed. Estelle C. Jelinek (Bloomington: Indiana Univ. Press, 1980), 163.
7 "Autogynography: Is the Subject Different?" in *The Female Autograph*, ed. Domna C. Stanton (Chicago: Univ. of Chicago Press, 1987), 11–13.
8 Ibid., 14–15.

to assume a similar degree of factuality with respect to the author's portrayal of Queen Elizabeth and herself. However, the one, probably deliberate, inaccuracy that has been found in the narrative should alert us to the possibility of others and make us mindful of Kottanner's motivation in telling her story. In fact, the narrator fashioned her story and created the two main characters, the queen and the servant, in view of a specific purpose and in accordance with the gender expectations and moral values of a specific audience. For what could be the significance of this famous "error" or lie? Kottanner describes in detail how following his enthronement in the Church of St. Peter and Paul, the infant King Ladislaus was carried in a festive procession through the coronation city Stuhlweissenburg. And while his mother's cousin, Count Ulrich Cillei, held the Holy Crown over the baby's head, other prominent nobles carried the royal insignia – the apple, the scepter, and the legate staff – "to show," says Kottanner, "that no part of Hungary is a fief of the Holy Roman Empire" (p. 44). However, at the time of the coronation, these royal insignia were either at the castle at Gran, where Albert had inspected them (pp. 21–22), or at the Plintenburg fortress, for although Kottanner does not explicitly mention their removal to Plintenburg along with the crowns, it is certainly logical to assume that they were taken there, since traditionally crowns and insignia were kept together.[9] But whether the insignia were in the castle at Gran or in the treasure vault of the Plintenburg, the point is that Kottanner knew full well that she and her Hungarian accomplice brought only the Holy Crown to the queen, and not the paraments. Hence, we must conclude either that no insignia were used at all – and perhaps Kottanner's mention of a legate "staff" when in fact it was a cross may be proof of this – or that Elizabeth used substitute insignia.[10] It is known that the original royal insignia were used for the coronation of the Polish Wladislaus a few months later. Yet Helene Kottanner wants her audience to believe that the regalia displayed during the coronation procession of the little Ladislaus were the authentic insignia of royal power in Hungary.

The passage follows almost directly upon a description of the coronation scene in which Kottanner particularly stresses the dynastic continuity and legality of Ladislaus' kingship: "Then the Archbishop took the Holy Crown and placed it on the head of the noblest king who ever lived in holy Christendom, King Lászlá, son of King Albert, grandson of Emperor Sigmund, who was crowned with the Holy Crown in

9 Karl Mollay, ed., *Die Denkwürdigkeiten der Helene Kottannerin (1439–1440)* (Vienna: Österreichische Bundesverlag, 1971), 50 n. 16; Erik Fügedi, *Kings, Bishops, Nobles and Burghers in Medieval Hungary* (London: Variorum, 1986), 1, 171.

10 See János M. Bak, *Königtum und Stände in Ungarn im 14.–16. Jahrhundert* (Wiesbaden: Franz Steiner Verlag, 1973), 170.

Stuhlweissenburg on the holy day of Pentecost by the Archbishop of Gran. For they have three laws in the kingdom of Hungary, and if a monarch fails to observe even one of them, the people refuse to acknowledge him as their rightful king. The first law requires that the king of Hungary be crowned with the Holy Crown. The second, that he be crowned by the Archbishop of Gran. The third, that the coronation take place in Stuhlweissenburg. All three laws were carefully observed in the case of the noble King Ladislaus . . ." (p. 43). The "laws" referred to here were customs rather than actual laws, but they certainly had the force of law.[11] Thus, Helene Kottanner demonstrates that Ladislaus Posthumous was indeed a truly legitimate Hungarian monarch, being both the son and the grandson of an Hungarian king and having respected all the rituals and rules of the Hungarian tradition. Her willingness to introduce a falsehood in her otherwise so accurate account by claiming that the regalia, too, were used at Ladislaus's coronation, suggests how important the question of his legitimacy was to Kottanner and her audience. But why?

Without further knowledge of the historical context, the reader may be tempted to conclude that the discussion of the three Hungarian "laws" seems addressed to the Hungarian barons who supported the Polish Wladislaus, at whose coronation, on 17 July 1440, the coronation of the little Ladislaus was declared null and void.[12] However, in 1452, the year in which most commentators think Helene Kottanner wrote or dictated her story, the legality of Ladislaus's kingship was no longer questioned; even Governor János Hunyadi referred to Ladislaus as "Dominus noster rex." And when in 1453 Ladislaus sent out messengers inviting the nobility of the country to his first Diet, the message read: ". . . in the thirteenth year of his reign."[13] Why then does the narrator insist so much on the legality of Ladislaus's kingship? Furthermore, what impelled Helene Kottanner to write these *Memoirs*, and to whom exactly are they addressed?

We know that on 17 March 1452 Johann Kottanner and his wife were granted the royal property Kisfalud on the peninsula that belonged to the city of Pressburg (now Bratislava). We know that the grant was made by János Hunyadi, who had been governor of Hungary since 1446. The Diet of that year had stipulated that as governor of the country Hunyadi had

---

11 See Fügedi, 1, 175–177; János Bak, *Konigtum und Stande*, 43.
12 Bak, ibid., 44.
13 János Hunyadi, Governor of Hungary during Ladislaus' absence and immaturity, officially handed over the power to the young king in 1453. See János Bak, *Königtum*, 52–53. On dating the Kottanner manuscript and the role of the Diet in Hungarian politics, see my introduction, 6–7 and 15–16.

all the rights and duties of a king, including the upper command of the army, but he was not allowed to make major gifts, and all his donations were subject to confirmation by the king.[14] This continued to be the case until 1453 when the Diet summoned by the young Ladislaus stipulated his rights and responsibilities as King of Hungary and also confirmed the donations made by Hunyadi.[15] Yet the Kottanners apparently did not actually take possession of their property until the grant had been confirmed by Ladislaus' successor, Matthias Corvinus, who was elected king in 1458.[16] This suggests that the *Memoirs* could have been written a few years later than has been thought and may actually be posterior to the document signed by Hunyadi, for the document itself did not guarantee a transfer of property. On the other hand, since Ladislaus Posthumous is undoubtedly one of the addressees of the *Memoirs*, the ante quo date must remain 1457, the year of his death.

Although Queen Elizabeth's son is never directly addressed in the text, one reference in particular provides a clue: immediately following the removal of the Holy Crown from the treasury, as Kottanner and her assistants carry the Holy Crown through the chapel of St. Elizabeth, she mentions her promise to donate a chasuble and an altar cloth "to be paid for by my gracious lord, King Ladislaus" (p. 31). This can mean one of two things: that Ladislaus himself must foot the bill for the promised objects or, perhaps more likely, considering what we know of Hunyadi's grant to the Kottanners, that Helene Kottanner needs to be paid by King Ladislaus before she can settle her debts. Hence, it is very likely that it was with the intention to incite King Ladislaus to finally impart to her the rewards promised long ago by his mother, Elizabeth, that Kottanner decided to reveal the details of the theft of the Crown and to recount the precarious circumstances of Ladislaus' birth, baptism and coronation.

That Ladislaus Posthumous, whose mother died when he was two and who had been raised at the court of Frederick III in Vienna, a virtual prisoner, far from those who had known him as an infant, should be interested in this story seems plausible. That the lengthy passages describing the little baby's fatigue and physical discomfort during the baptism, the journey to Stuhlweissenburg, the coronation, and later the journey to Ödenburg are meant to elicit the sympathies of the young king, who was no more than thirteen or fourteen years old at the time, is very likely too. Conventional chronicles, even those containing descriptive passages such as Thuróczy's *Chronicle of Hungary*, did not bother with information of

---

14 Bak, *Königtum*, 51.
15 Ibid., 53.
16 See the introduction, 3.

this nature, nor would the adult men surrounding the king be interested in these details.

However, when Kottanner explains that Ladislaus's birth one week earlier than calculated was a "miracle" willed by God, she seems to be addressing someone other than the king: "But if it is true that the Holy Crown was sent to the Holy Saint Stephen by God and meant by God for him, it is also true that it was clearly God's will that the true heir, King Lászlá, and not the King of Poland, should receive the Holy Crown of Hungary. There are certain people who ought to remember that" (p. 35). Like the passage containing the lie, this passage also seems addressed to the Hungarian barons who supported the polish Wladislaus. In Kottanner's view, they not only made a political mistake, they also failed to see that God supported Elizabeth and that Ladislaus's kingship, as opposed to that of Wladislaus, was divinely ordained. Nevertheless, Kottanner's insistence on the validity of Ladislaus's kingship as being in accordance with both Hungarian and divine law, at a time when the boy's claims were not in dispute, remains puzzling. Perhaps this means that the text was written later than has generally been thought, namely after the death of the legendary and immensely popular János Hunyadi, when Ladislaus's renewed strained relations with the Hunyadi party and particularly the hero's two sons, Ladislaus and Matthias, caused Hungarians to resent the Austrian Habsburger once more as a "foreigner."

This happened in the fall and spring of the years 1456–1457. During a visit to Belgrade, main fortress of the Hunyadi clan, Count Ulrich Cillei, Ladislaus's ambitious uncle, was knifed down. Under pressure from the Hunyadi party, King Ladislaus first guaranteed impunity to the murderers of his uncle but later had both sons imprisoned, and on 16 March 1457 the twenty-three-year-old Ladislaus Hunyadi was killed. Apparently, Matthias was condemned to death but later pardoned. A modern expert on that period of Hungarian history concludes: "This conduct of the 'foreign' king with respect to the sons of the great defeater of the Turks, Hunyadi, caused unrest, so that shortly thereafter Ladislaus had to leave Hungary." [17]

The young King Ladislaus died on 23 November 1457, less than six months after leaving Hungary, in the face of a growing wave of anti-Habsburg sentiment. The Diet of 1458 elected as his successor the young Matthias Hunyadi, whose surname had become, among the county nobility and in the large Hungarian territories belonging to his family, synonymous with protest against the "foreign" Habsburg king.[18] It seems to me

[17] Bak, *Königtum*, 110–111. My translation.
[18] Ibid., 54.

that Helene Kottanner's insistence on the validity of King Ladislaus and
Queen Elizabeth as *Hungarian* monarchs is understandable only in light
of these events. Since she still had not been allowed to take possession of
the property that Hunyadi had promised her, Helene Kottanner turned for
help to King Ladislaus but also to the Hungarian nobles on whose support
his power in Hungary depended.[19]

Her intended audience, the queen's son and his political (and financial)
backers, and her implied purpose, self-promotion and self-justification in
view of obtaining a promised reward, explain certain technical features
of the narrative. For one, the absence of physical description; details of
physique or physiognomy are unnecessary, for the characters are for the
most part familiar to the audience. Secondly, since Kottanner's audience
was largely illiterate and used to straightforward oral narration, she told
her story in the manner of oral recollection, in chronological order, with,
at regular intervals, rhetorical questions and direct appeals to the
reader/listener and references forward and backward in time which link
the events logically, accelerate the rhythm, and create narrative cohesion.

Another aspect of the text which is no doubt directly related to the
narrator's purpose and intended audience is the complete absence of any
timidity about the fact of writing itself. Although much writing by
women, past and present, is characterized by a "defensive or justificative
posture," marking a subject fearful to usurp the (traditionally male)
prerogative of writing, there is no such authorial self-consciousness in
Kottanner's *Memoirs*.[20] Nor does the narrator lack self-confidence. The
few instances of ostensible humility in the text actually achieve the
opposite effect, pointing up the narrator's pride in her strong position at
court and exceptional relationship with the queen. This self-confidence

---

[19] It is true, as Reiffenstein has argued, that we do not know if the *Memoirs* were originally
longer and if so, which political events were included in the lost portion of the manuscript.
It is also true that the queen's Austrian supporters, Duke Albert, Ulrich Cillei, and especially
Kottanner's guide and protector, Ulrich von Eitzing, are treated with great respect and
admiration by the narrator. This has led at least one critic to conclude that they and not the
young Ladislaus are the addressees of the *Memoirs*. Yet it is not clear what effective
assistance these Austrian nobles could have given Helene Kottanner in the early 1450s.
Moreover, these Austrian supporters of Queen Elizabeth attended the coronation festivities
and hence knew the truth about the regalia, nor did they need to be convinced of the legality
of Ladislaus's claims to the Hungarian throne.

It does not seem likely to me that Kottanner wrote primarily to defend the legal and
political claims of the young king, for his claims, in the years 1452–1453 at least, were not
in question. Rather, the particular audience with which Helene Kottanner sought to ingratiate
herself was composed of the young King Ladislaus and the powerful Hungarian magnates
without whose political support his kingship was meaningless. For a contrasting opinion,
see Ingo Reiffenstein's review of Mollay's edition of Kottanner's manuscript in *Sprachkunst*
4 (1973) 1–2: 164–166.

[20] Domna Stanton, 13.

is striking, considering that in addition to the young Ladislaus Kottanner was addressing a potentially hostile adult male audience.

While the boy Ladislaus may have welcomed the opportunity to learn more about his long-deceased mother, some of his Hungarian supporters had probably known the queen personally and may not have been favorably disposed toward her, for Queen Elizabeth had not been popular in Hungary. To counter this, Kottanner presents the queen from the perspective of someone who knows her better than anyone else, the privileged, intimate perspective of a trusted servant and confidante. Thus, her portrayal of the queen as ambitious, calculating, and clever – characteristics unlikely to endear her to this audience – is balanced by frequent references to the queen's wisdom, her anguish and doubt, her concern for her family, and genuine faith in God, aspects which Kottanner's close association with the queen would have allowed her to know about and present convincingly.

In studying Helene Kottanner's portrayal of Queen Elizabeth and herself it is important to keep in mind that she meant to please and persuade, not shock or alienate, her male audience. Hence we can expect her to have toned down or smoothed over potentially irritating features of the characters as they were known to their contemporaries and emphasized or added qualities that would make the portraits conform to conventional notions of female virtue. In view of her purpose it would have been unwise to risk aggravating her audience or, worse, being dismissed as ridiculous or irrelevant by challenging the prevailing role expectations for men and women. This is clear in Kottanner's portrayal of the queen but even more evident in the way she portrays herself.

Queen Elizabeth is presented as a capable monarch who would have made a successful regent in Hungary. She has impeccable credentials, great "wisdom," and political skill. Both her father and her husband were kings of Hungary, she understands and speaks the language, knows and respects the customs and traditions, and has her son crowned king despite major adversity. Her ordering the theft of the Holy Crown for this purpose is motivated by her deep concern for dynastic continuity in Hungary, Kottanner shows, not thirst for power.

That the queen was too busy with her affairs, or too indifferent, to return to her ailing husband shortly before he died even though he had repeatedly expressed the wish to see her, elicits no more than a note of faint regret on Kottanner's part: a last visit of Elizabeth's to Albert "would have been in the interest of both" (p. 23). His death is not shown to have had any emotional impact on his wife, nor does his funeral in Stuhlweissenburg have a place in the narrative. That Elizabeth was supported in her ambitions by only a minority of Hungarian prelates and barons and

pushed her claims even though the principle of elective kingship repre-
sented by Wladislaus was supported by the majority – something the
politically astute Kottanner must have known – is not part of the story
either. Nor does the narrator conceal the fact that Elizabeth planned to
hold on to power, whether the child turned out to be a boy or a girl
(p. 26).[21] This side of the character corresponds with what is known of
Elizabeth's reputation at the time and therefore would have confirmed the
intended audience's image of Ladislaus's mother. However, through her
privileged position as personal assistant, councillor and, in some respects,
"partner in crime," the narrator convincingly adds another dimension
which makes the "wise and noble" queen both admirable and sympa-
thetic.

Her superior judgment and sincere devotion to the cause of Hungary
are emphasized throughout. Hence, when she and her advisors heed the
warning of an unnamed Hungarian lord who claims that Albert before his
death had secretly moved the Holy Crown to an unknown location, the
narrator calls this "wise," rather than evidence of Elizabeth's distrust of
her husband, although the rumor later proved to be unfounded. Her
feigned willingness to marry Wladislaus on three (unfulfillable) conditions is "wise" and points up the lesser political savvy of the Hungarian
magnates, "who did not see through this" (p. 26). Again, with her "great
wisdom" the queen realized that it was safer for her and the baby to stay
in the lower castle of the Plintenburg stronghold instead of her own palace
at the top of the stronghold. And she carefully plans the abduction of the
Holy Crown far ahead of time, making sure that Kottanner's return to the
fortress will arouse no suspicion. Again and again, the narrator praises
the queen's wisdom in not showing her true feelings or thoughts (cf. pp.
38, 47), for her survival, and that of the baby king, depend on shrewd
calculation and self-control as well as self-denial and self-sacrifice.

"Burdened with many problems and beset by many worries" (p. 25),
the queen is shown to suffer from the weight of her responsibilities, ever
mindful of the dangers surrounding her and her family, and described in
her intimate conversations with Kottanner as troubled, saddened, or
distressed (for example, pp. 25, 28, 36). When safety considerations make
it imperative for the royal family to separate and travel in different
directions, the queen, usually confident and composed in public, shakes
as she says good-bye to her children and to her trusted confidante (p. 51).
Her despair and loss of self-control, so soon after the triumph of the
coronation, are clearly meant to move. And so are the queen's meekness

---

[21] According to Fügedi, Queen Elizabeth had no designs on the Hungarian throne but changed
her mind once she learned that the baby was a boy. Cf. 1, 172.

and gratitude following Ladislaus's birth. These signs of doubt, humility and maternal tenderness make the queen, if not altogether likeable, certainly admirable and worthy of sympathy and understanding. Thus, Kottanner has created a rather positive image with which her portrayal of herself, the queen's servant and closest associate, is implicitly compared.

Unfolding at the same time as the story of the theft of the crown and of Kottanner's services to Queen Elizabeth and her children is the story of the development of the relationship between the two women. The former serves to demonstrate Kottanner's presence of mind and resourcefulness, her power and authority at court, her insight and knowledge in many areas, and her great loyalty to the queen, the king, and the Holy Crown. The latter shows the growing intimacy between the queen and herself, their mutual understanding, their essential equality despite vast differences of class and situation, and Kottanner's significance, and superiority, as the very embodiment of motherliness.

Though but a servant and a "humble woman" (p. 44), Kottanner portrays herself as having a sort of natural authority that is respected by the queen's aristocratic female assistants, the ladies-in-waiting, as well as by the noblemen in her entourage. Asked by the queen to make sure that the Holy Crown is safe, Counts Nicholas and George of Pösing first check with Kottanner before examining the seals on the treasury door in her presence (p. 23). Important nobles such as the Great Count and Duke Albert treat her with respect. That she may have been, in the queen's female entourage, a force to be reckoned with, jealously guarding her privileged position and perhaps even controlling the queen's accessibility to others, is suggested by the annoyed reaction of the two widows, Lady Siebenlinder and Lady Zauzach, who had come from Ofen bringing with them their own mid-wife and a nurse to assist the queen during labor. They had missed the birth and "strongly suspected that this was my doing," concedes Kottanner, who then immediately defends herself by saying that there simply had not been enough time to send for them, since their lodgings were on the other side of town (p. 35). But whatever resentment of Kottanner's influence with the queen there may have been, it was overshadowed, she demonstrates, by a general respect for and confidence in her abilities. The queen's advisors all agree that Helene Kottanner is the best person to accompany and take care of the little king. And during the journey, Ulrich von Eitzing, an influential nobleman, does not object when Kottanner acts on behalf of the queen and asks him to order his soldiers to return the lifestock they have stolen. Thus Kottanner shows that she equaled or surpassed her superiors in practical sense, influence with the queen, and authority.

She also shows that she is extremely knowledgeable. She knows about chronology and geography, politics and law, medicine and gynecology. When examining the queen upon her return from the Plintenburg stronghold, she apparently recognizes the signs that indicate that the birth of the child is imminent and tells the queen to get ready for labor. And indeed the baby is born within the hour.[22] According to Kottanner, the ladies who were with the queen, at least one of whom was married, "knew nothing about such matters" (p. 34). Is it a wonder, then, that this bearer of worldly knowledge and divine truth is the one who holds the keys and brings light, in the form of candles and a torch?

Kottanner's knowledge and ability to think clearly are recognized by the queen who repeatedly comes to her for advice, particularly concerning the safety of the Holy Crown (for example, pp. 39, 46–47) and her children. In fact, the queen's request for advice as to where to send her children and who to send along with them marks the high point both of their relationship and of Kottanner's position at court: "What do you advise, dear mother Kottanner? If I could divide you in three parts, I would gladly do it. I would like to keep you for myself, and I would also like to leave you with my son, and I would also like to see you staying with my daughter" (p. 49). Thus, the humble servant has become indispensable to the royal family. That she serves her queen willingly, but at the expense of great anguish and suffering, is stressed throughout. Stealing the Holy Crown "meant great danger for me and my little children" (p. 27). She fears for her body as well as her soul and is tortured by restless dreams and sleepless nights. This suffering becomes worse when Kottanner is chosen to accompany the little king on his journey to Ödenburg and hence is deprived of the queen's company.

Yet this devotion in no way implies subservience. Far from it. When the queen suggests that it might be better to return the stolen crown to the treasure vault again, she incurs Kottanner's unmitigated wrath: "Woman, stop that! I will not do it and will not risk my life like that and will not even help you with advise, for it is always better to be in the bushes than in the stocks" (p. 39). It is a measure of the two women's sense of their essential equality that the queen quietly accepts this reprimand. Similarly, following the birth of the baby, when the mid-wife and all other women have left the room, Kottanner reminds the queen of her obligations to God, urging her, much like a mother might do, to "thank God as long as you live for the great mercy and the miracle which God Almighty has bestowed on us by bringing the king and the Holy Crown together within the same hour" (pp. 34–35).

The fundamental equality of Queen Elizabeth and her servant is

[22] See 34 n. 38.

evident even in the balanced way in which Kottanner composed the characters. For example, the two women have parallel responses to Kottanner's ominous dreams: when she dreams that a woman has penetrated into the vault and carried off the Holy Crown, Kottanner gets out of bed immediately to check on the door to the vault (p. 32); and when she dreams that the Holy Crown has fallen into a dirt pit and tells the queen about it, Elizabeth rushes to the place where the Crown is hidden and examines it carefully (p. 49). Moreover, two errors or moments of failure are given for each character. Kottanner misjudges the Croatian nobleman she first selects as her assistant (p. 27). Later she recommends that they bury the Crown in the garden of the Brobsthof, which the queen considers a mistake. Similarly, the queen misjudges the situation when she meets the supporters of the Polish Wladislaus in front of her castle rather than inside, for this turns out to be very dangerous (p. 38), and in a moment of confusion she wonders if she shouldn't return the Holy Crown to Plintenburg, which Kottanner rejects as foolish (p. 39).

The ultimate proof of their fundamental equality is given, however, when the queen, in a reversal of roles, listens to her servant and comforts her (p. 50), more importantly, when Kottanner is the only person in the entire royal household who is not required to swear an oath of loyalty (p. 50). Thus the queen and her servant emerge as equal partners joined by a common purpose and the secret they share who outshine and outwit the enemy. Standing together on the battlements of the Komorn castle, with Kottanner holding the torch to light up the darkness of early dawn, they represent special knowledge and a higher cause. Repeatedly the narrator asserts: "nobody knows but God, except her grace and myself" (pp. 26, 47).

This auto-portrait of Kottanner as a woman intelligent, influential, nimbly moving across social and sexual barriers, and wise in the ways of God and the world, is completed, and at the same time also tempered, by pervasive references to her motherliness. In fact, images of her in a maternal or Madonna-like posture abound. She is repeatedly portrayed with on her arm the little princess Elizabeth, whom she raised and who, as everyone at court apparently knows, is very attached to her (for example, p. 28). Later, after the birth of Ladislaus Posthumous, it is him she carries in her arms, not only while traveling but also during all important events involving the baby: his baptism, confirmation, enthronement and the coronation procession. Moreover, observations such as the one about the little Elizabeth who during the coronation ceremony had been placed upstairs, by the organ, "so she would not get hurt in the crowd" (p. 43), bespeak the watchfulness of a motherly eye.

Indeed, Kottanner is promoting an image of herself as the quintessential Mother. This impression is reinforced in other ways, for example through the address forms used for her by the other characters. Except once, when in her anguish she dispenses with address forms altogether (p. 46), the queen always addresses Kottanner as "dear mother Kottanner" (pp. 24, 39, 49, 50). Ladislaus Garai, who may be suspicious of her, calls her by her full name (p. 27), and her Hungarian helper, who speaks no German, addresses her simply as "Woman" (p. 29), but the powerful Great Count and the highly respected Ulrich von Eitzing both call her "mother Kottanner" (pp. 37, 51).[23] The narrator also notes that the queen, out of gratitude, wants Helene Kottanner to be her son's godmother, a distinction which the servant, however, knowing her place, declines; she shrewdly refers Queen Elizabeth to the noble Lady Margit as a more suitable candidate (p. 35).

It is an essential feature of Kottanner's narrative strategy that the feminine and maternal posture dominates in some of the scenes in which she is most prominently profiled. She is the one who *sews* all the different parts of the child's minute costume in preparation for the coronation; and on the way to the coronation city it is she who rides in front with the young king, while the queen and her daughter ride in the back. Thus, she literally leads the way, heading the royal retinue, but always in a maternal posture, carrying the baby in her arms. Something similar happens when Kottanner has to carry the child into a circle of mounted knights holding naked swords in their hands; rather than King Ladislaus we visualize Helene Kottanner as the Madonna with Child at the center of the circle. This emphasis on the maternal character of Kottanner's participation in the events serves to show that rather than overstepping conventional class and gender boundaries, she has stayed firmly within the traditional framework and performed only to the best of her not inconsiderable abilities the role assigned to her by God and Mother Nature, and that it is especially because she was a better mother to the little Elizabeth and Ladislaus than the queen herself that she deserves to be granted her reward.

Queen Elizabeth herself promised to reward Helene Kottanner on two different occasions – or so the narrator claims. In the text, the two passages again illustrate the increasing mutuality and equality of the relationship between the two women, and the second promise reinforces the first. Following the coronation, when her work as "thief" of the Holy Crown has had the desired result, Helene Kottanner kneels down in front of the queen in the manner expected of a servant and reminds her of all she has

---

23 Even if "mother" was frequently used to address older female servants in general, that does not diminish the effect of this address form in Kottanner's *Memoirs*.

done for the royal family. Responding in the manner expected of a queen, mindful of their different stations in life, Elizabeth orders her servant to stand up and promises: "If it happens that God grants that everything goes well and our difficulties are resolved, I will elevate you and all your family. You have truly deserved that, for you have done for me and my children more than I would have been capable or in the position to do myself" (p. 45). The second time the queen needs no prodding but volunteers a promise in response to Kottanner's obvious anguish at their impending separation; she vows to "share" with Kottanner even her very last penny (p. 50).

Interestingly, the narrator is unable to produce witnesses who could testify to the truth of these two crucial passages, ostensibly because the conversations took place in private. Perhaps this is the reason why she is so anxious elsewhere to advance witnesses and evidence to corroborate her story. Not only does she emphasize, again and again, that she herself was there and saw everything with her own eyes – this in itself is a strong truth claim which would have carried considerable weight in an oral culture – she repeatedly establishes additional truth value for her account by referring to facts that are "well known" (for example, p. 22), by pointing to concrete proof, such as the files used to open the vault which she threw in the privy "where you will find them . . . as proof that I am speaking the truth" (p. 31), by mentioning the people, often by name, who were with her, as during the scene of the fire in the ladies' bedroom (p. 24), or when she had a bad dream and took a lady, "whose name *is* Dachpeck," she says, using the present tense, and who is hence perhaps still alive at the time of writing, with her to check on the door to the vault (p. 32). She even accounts for witnesses who might contradict certain aspects of her story. For example, the old woman servant she had with her during the night of the theft, "who did not know a word of German and who also knew nothing of our plan and was unfamiliar with the castle," who "lay there and was fast asleep" (p. 29). And her unnamed Hungarian helper, who never learned of the mysterious sounds she heard and the miracles that happened while he worked in the vault and she kept watch outside, for she does not speak Hungarian and "he did not know much German and there was no one I could trust who could have translated for me" (p. 33). Thus Kottanner attempts to convince her audience of the truth of the queen's promises by making them plausible in the context of her special relationship with the queen and believable by virtue of the demonstrated truth value of the rest of the story. Nevertheless, her efforts to pre-empt possible accusations of inaccuracy or mendacity seem somewhat excessive, as if she were trying to suppress a guilty conscience. Would her contemporaries have questioned the truth of the queen's alleged promises? To judge by Hunyadi's grant, Kottanner's claims were considered valid by the relevant parties.

This general impression of verisimilitude and reliability effected on the one hand by narrative plausibility and on the other hand by the narrator's recourse to witnesses and tangible evidence is reinforced by frequent references to her faith, her relationship with God and her conviction that God supports Elizabeth. In fact, Kottanner demonstrates that whatever happened, including the mistakes and accidents that seemed to threaten the happy outcome of the queen's scheme, was willed and planned by God. The story of Elizabeth's triumph and decline is viewed throughout from the perspective of divine providence, that Eternal Divine Plan that determines the movements and meaning of history. In this respect, the *Memoirs* of Helene Kottanner resemble traditional medieval historiography, their overall "emplotment" of history being essentially identical to that of the medieval chronicle.

In light of her purpose in telling this story, it would be tempting to think, as an unadvised modern reader might, that Helene Kottanner used this conventional "emplotment" to serve her own ends, and indeed, in some respects, this may be so, for demonstrating the divine patronage of Elizabeth's cause certainly would not hurt her own. Yet, it would be erroneous to conclude that this late-medieval woman did not sincerely believe in the divine origin of the "miracles" and "miraculous deeds" (for example, pp. 24, 28, 32–33, 34–35), the mysterious sounds during the night of the theft, or her two dreams about the Holy Crown (pp. 32, 49). Her faith is genuine and genuinely medieval; God and the Devil fight out their differences over the heads of human beings and directly interfere in their affairs. And while the Devil sides with the queen's enemies, God protects and helps Elizabeth.

Therefore, accidents, curious incidents, visions and dreams are given a religious and spiritual rather than psychological interpretation. When one of the queen's ladies-in-waiting inadvertently knocks over a burning candle and the fire that flares up almost reaches the royal crowns, the narrator observes that though the Holy Crown and the future king were only two cords away from one another and both in close proximity to the flames, the Devil was powerless and could not harm them, because "God watched over us and awakened the ladies in time" (p. 24). Later, while the Hungarian and his assistant are laboring with files and hammer to break open the seals and locks on the door to the treasure vault, Kottanner, who in an adjacent room lies prostrate begging God for mercy, suddenly hears the din of armored men at the door. She interrupts her prayers to see who is there but finds the place deserted. This happens several times (for example, pp. 30–31).

In post-Freudian times, phenomena such as these are explained as products of the woman's own feverish and guilty conscience, but Kottanner can only attribute them to evil forces and turns the incident into evidence of the Devil's attempts to foil the queen's, and hence God's, plan. Likewise, she interprets her two dreams about the Holy Crown as messages of warning sent to her by God. Contrary to the modern view of dreams as manifestations primarily of the human mind, medieval people saw most, though not all, dreams as messages from a genuinely existing world outside them; "God himself, his angels and saints, but also the demons sent people messages, of warning, injunction, or revelation."[24] Hence Helene Kottanner focuses on the warning of danger and is not bothered by the fact that in the first dream it is a *woman* who penetrates through the wall and steals the Holy Crown (p. 32).

This may be an instance where modern psychology enables us to perceive reflections of the inner life of a late-medieval woman of which she herself could not be aware. For it is not at all unlikely that Kottanner's dreams were influenced by the spiritual anguish that is manifest throughout the story. During the fearful hours of the night of the theft, she is tortured by doubt and the threat of damnation: "I feared more for my soul than for my life, and I begged God that if the undertaking were against His will, I should be damned for it; or if something evil should result for the country and the people, that God have mercy on my soul and let me die here on the spot" (p. 30). This passage as well as the dream just discussed suggest that Kottanner may have been subject to a guilty conscience and that her guilt was associated with the theft of the Holy Crown, in other words that she may not have been completely sure, after all, that God endorsed Elizabeth's plan. Maybe she knew that the Holy Crown had been stolen once before, in the early fourteenth century, and that at that time the adherents of the culprit had been excommunicated by the Archbishop of Esztergom.[25] At any rate, the second dream, in which the Crown has fallen into a dirt pit, could be interpreted as being symbolic of Kottanner's own unconscious sense that the Holy Crown of St. Stephen has become soiled and debased by what has happened to it and that she is responsible for that. It seems to me, therefore, that the *Memoirs*, in addition to being a document of self-promotion intended to stimulate the generosity of Ladislaus V and his Hungarian backers (this is the intentional and manifest content), became also, unconsciously, in the course of writing, an attempt on the part of the narrator to justify the theft to

---

[24] Peter Dinzelbacher in *Träume im Mittelalter*, ed. Agostino Paravicini Bagliani and Giorgio Stabile (Stuttgart: Belser Verlag, 1989), 163.

[25] Fügedi, 1: 179.

herself and to God and thus to pacify a burdened and restless conscience (the unintentional, latent, more truly autobiographical content).

Given the way Kottanner profiles herself in the text as the very embodiment of maternal tenderness and solicitude, we may wonder whether she felt any guilt with respect to her own family and whether, in fact, guilt rather than calculation might have motivated her insistence on the maternal nature of her involvement throughout. However, if this were so, then she suppressed her feelings successfully. Only twice does she refer to her own children: once in the beginning, upon learning of the queen's intentions ("This frightened me, for it meant great danger for me and my little children," p. 27), and once toward the end, when she is appointed to accompany the king (". . . I also had to leave behind my husband and my daughter Katharina," p. 51). Her husband is mentioned in only one more instance, when she notes, with obvious pride about her own more privileged position with the queen, that while he too occupied an important place in the royal household, he like everyone else except his wife "had to swear loyalty on the reliquary" (p. 50). If she felt any compunction about her failure to consult him or initiate him into her secret, she absolutely does not show it. In fact, the "systematic tension" or conflict between public and private, self and others, that has been found to be so prevalent in women's autobiographies, is completely absent here.[26] Kottanner's portrayal of herself as mainly motherly and maternal may have agreed to some extent with her own gender values and no doubt helped in the process of clearing her conscience and justifying herself before God, but it was consciously conceived, I think, as a device designed to manipulate the gender expectations of her intended audience, the young orphaned king and the Hungarian barons who supported him.

Clearly, here too, in the autobiographical triad of "the self, the life, and the writing," the "I" is someone else, a fiction, and the "life" is created by the writing. Yet the signature – I, Helene Kottanner – cannot be dissociated from the subjective self that transpires and asserts itself in spite of the narrator's pragmatic intentions, from the bits and pieces, reflections and refractions, of the inner world of a woman who delights in her accomplishments but perhaps unconsciously doubts their morality; who accepts the class system and her own social position yet glories in demonstrating her superiority over the aristocratic ladies-in-waiting and her essential equality with the queen; who seems to subscribe to the traditional division of labor between men and women yet triumphs in her independence, strength of will, and the historical significance of her role, having actively influenced the course of events in Hungary; who has a

[26] See Stanton, 13–14.

husband and children yet apparently feels in no way limited or restricted by family responsibilities; the irrepressible "I" of the woman who says: "as *I* was talking to the noble queen like this," when, in fact, as she had just shown us, the queen was talking to her (p. 33).

Bibliography

Bagliani, Agostino Paravicini, and Giorgio Stabile, eds. *Träume Im Mittelalter*. Stuttgart: Belser Verlag, 1989.

Bak, János M. *Coronations: Medieval and Early Modern Monarchic Ritual*. Berkeley: Univ. of California Press, 1990.

Bak, János M. *Königtum und Stände in Ungarn im 14–16. Jahrhundert*. Wiesbaden: Franz Steiner Verlag, 1973.

Bennett, Judith M., and Elizabeth A. Clark, Jean F. O'Barr, B. Anne Vilen, Sarah Westphal-Wihl, eds. *Sisters and Workers in the Middle Ages*. Chicago: Univ. of Chicago Press, 1989.

Bennett, Judith M. "History that Stands Still: Women's Work in the European Past." *Feminist Studies*, 14:2 (Summer 1988): 269–283.

Bijvoet, Maya C. "Helene Kottanner: The Austrian Chambermaid." In *Women Writers of the Renaissance and Reformation*, ed. K. M. Wilson, 327–349. Athens: Univ. of Georgia Press, 1987.

Bilson, Marcus K., and Sidonie A. Smith. "Lilian Hellman and the Strategy of the Other." In *Women's Autobiography*, ed. Estelle C. Jelinek. Bloomington: Indiana Univ. Press, 1980.

Daniel, David P. "Piety, Politics and Perversion: Noblewomen in Reformation Hungary." In *Women in Reformation and Counter-Reformation Europe*, ed. Sherrin Marshall. Bloomington: Indiana Univ. Press, 1989.

Davis, Natalie Zemon. "Gender and Genre: Women as Historical Writers 1400–1820." In *Beyond Their Sex: Learned Women of the European Past*, ed. Labalme, 153–183. New York, 1980.

Davis, Natalie Zemon. "Women on Top." In *Society and Culture in Early Modern France*, 124–151. Palo Alto: Stanford Univ. Press, 1975.

Doderer, Heimito von. "Helene Kottanner: Denkwürdigkeiten einer Wienerin von 1440." In *Die Wiederkehr der Drachen*, 221–226. Munich, 1970.

Doderer, Heimito von. *Die Dämonen*. Munich, 1956.

Engel, Pál. Preface to Thuróczy's *Chronicle of the Hungarians*, 1–20. Bloomington: Indiana Univ. Press, 1991.

Engelmann, M., ed. *Aus den Denkwürdigkeiten der Helene Kottannerin*. Leipzig, 1846.

Fisher, Sheila, and Janet E. Halley. "The Lady Vanishes: The Problem of Women's Absence in Late Medieval and Renaissance Texts." In *Seeking the Woman in Late Medieval and Renaissance Writings*, 1–17. Knoxville: Univ. of Tennessee Press, 1989.

Freytag, Gustav. *Bilder aus der deutschen Vergangenheit*, Bd 2, 370–382. Leipzig, 1924.

Fügedi, Erik. *Kings, Bishops, Nobles and Burghers in Medieval Hungary*, ed. J. M. Bak. London: Variorum, 1986.

Ganshof, F. L. *Feudalism*. New York: Harper & Row, 1961.

Grossmann, Karl, ed. Jakob Unrest's *Österreichische Chronik*. Munich: Monumenta Germiniae Historica, 1957. repr. 1982.

Gusdorf, Georges. "Conditions and Limits of Autobiography." In *Autobiography: Essays Theoretical and Critical*, ed. J. Olney, 27–43. Princeton: Princeton Univ. Press, 1980.

Hanawalt, Barbara A., ed. *Women and Work in Preindustrial Europe*. Bloomington: Indiana Univ. Press, 1986.

Herlihy, David. *Opera Muliebra: Women and Work in Medieval Europe*. Philadelphia: Temple Univ. Press, 1990.

Herlihy, David. *The History of Feudalism*. New York: Harper & Row, 1970

Howell, Martha, Suzanne Wemple and Denise Kaiser. "A Documented Presence: Medieval Women in Germanic Historiography." In *Women in Medieval History and Historiography*, ed. Susan Mosher Stuard, 101–131. Philadelphia: Univ. of Pennsylvania Press, 1987

Howell, Martha C. *Women, Production and Patriarchy in Late Medieval Cities*. Chicago: Univ. of Chicago Press, 1986.

Jacobsen, Grethe. "Pregnancy and childbirth in the Medieval North." *Scandinavian Journal of History* 9:2 (1984): 91–111.

Jelinek, Estelle C. *The Tradition of Women's Autobiography*. Boston: Twayne, 1986.

Jelinek, Estelle C., ed. *Women's Autobiography: Essays in Criticism*. Bloomington: Indiana Univ. Press, 1980.

Kilényi, Maria. *Könnyek és Korona*. Budapest, 1947.

Kottanner, Helene. *Die Denkwürdigkeiten der Helene Kottannerin 1439–1440*, ed. Karl Mollay. Vienna: Österreichischer Bundesverlag, 1971.

Kraemer, Ross S. "The Conversion of Women to Ascetic Forms of Christianity." In *Sisters and Workers in the Middle Ages*, ed. Judith Bennett et al., 198–207. Chicago: Chicago Univ. Press, 1989.

Lemay, Helen. "Women and the Literature of Obstetrics and Gynecology." In *Medieval Women and the Sources of Medieval History*, ed. Joel T. Rosenthal, 189–210. Athens: Univ. of Georgia Press, 1990.

Liebertz-Grün, Ursula. "Frau und Herrscherin." In *Auf der Suche nach der Frau im Mittelalter*, ed. Bea Lundt. Munich: Wilhelm Fink Verlag, 1991.

Liebertz-Grün, Ursula. "Höfische Autorinnen von der karolingischen Kulturreform bis zum Humanismus." In *Deutsche Literatur von Frauen*, Bd. 1, ed. Gisela Brinker-Gabler, 39–64. Munich: C. H. Beck, 1988.

Liebertz-Grün, Ursula. "Autorinnen im Umkreis der Höfe." In *Frauen Literatur Geschichte*, ed. Hiltrud Gnüg and Renate Mohrmann, 16–34. Stuttgart: J. B. Metzlersche Verlagsbuchhandlung, 1985.

Macartney, C. A. *Hungary*. Edinburgh: Edinburgh Univ. Press, 1953.

Marshall, Sherrin, ed. *Women in Reformation and Counter-Reformation Europe*. Bloomington: Indiana Univ. Press, 1989.

Mason, Mary G. "The Other Voice: Autobiographies of Women Writers." In *Autobiography: Essays Theoretical and Critical*, ed. James Olney, 207–221. Princeton: Princeton Univ. Press, 1980.

Mollay, Karl, ed. *Die Denkwürdigkeiten der Helene Kottannerin 1439–1440*. Vienna: Österreichischer Bundesverlag, 1971.

Olney, James, ed. *Autobiography: Essays Theoretical and Critical*. Princeton: Princeton Univ. Press, 1980.

Reiffenstein, Ingo. Review of Mollay's edition of Kottanner. *Sprachkunst* 4 (1973) 1–2: 164–166.

Rosenthal, Joel T., ed. *Medieval Women and the Sources of Medieval History*. Athens: Univ. of Georgia Press, 1990.

Rupprich, Hans. "Das Wiener Schrifttum des ausgehenden Mittelalters." *Österreichische Akademie der Wissenschaften* 228, no. 5 (1954).

Stanton, Domna C., ed. *The Female Autograph: Theory and Practise of Autobiography*. Chicago: Univ. of Chicago Press, 1987.

Stuard, Susan Mosher, ed. *Women in Medieval History and Historiography*. Philadelphia: Univ. of Pennsylvania Press, 1987.

Sugar, Peter, Péter Hanák and Tibor Frank, eds. *A History of Hungary*. Bloomington: Indiana Univ. Press, 1990.

Thuróczy, János. *Chronicle of the Hungarians*, trans. Frank Mantello. Bloomington: Indiana Univ. Press, 1991.

Uitz, Erika. *Women in the Medieval Town*. London: Barrie & Jenkins.

Unrest, Jacob. *Österreichische Chronik*, ed. Karl Grossmann. Munich: Monumenta Germaniae Historica, 1957. repr. 1982.

Wengraf, Alice. "Aus den Denkwürdigkeiten der Helene Kottannerin." *Ungarische Rundschau* 3:8 (1970): 438–441.

Wiesner, Merry E. *Working Women in Renaissance Germany*. New Brunswick: Rutgers Univ. Press, 1986.

Wilson, Katharina M., ed. *Women Writers of the Renaissance and Reformation*. Athens: Univ. of Georgia Press, 1987.

Zeman, Herbert. "Österreichische Literatur: Zwei Studien." *Jahrbuch der Grillparzer-Gesellschaft* 3:8 (1970): 17–18.

Index